The Nelson Guide to Good English

The Nelson Guide to Good
English

Denys Thompson

Nelson

Thomas Nelson and Sons Ltd
Lincoln Way Windmill Road Sunbury-on-Thames Middlesex TW16 7HP
P.O. Box 73146 Nairobi Kenya

Thomas Nelson (Australia) Ltd
19–39 Jeffcott Street West Melbourne Victoria 3003

Thomas Nelson and Sons (Canada) Ltd
81 Curlew Drive Don Mills Ontario

Thomas Nelson (Nigeria) Ltd
8 Ilupeju Bypass PMB 1303 Ikeja Lagos

© Denys Thompson 1976
First published 1976
ISBN 0 17 443303 4

Printed in Great Britain by
Whitstable Litho Ltd., Whitstable, Kent

Acknowledgements

For permission to reprint copyright material
grateful acknowledgements are due to:
Jacquetta Hawkes and Barrie & Jenkins — *A Land*;
M. L. Peters and Routledge & Kegan Paul Ltd —
Spelling: Caught or Taught; Vance Packard and
The Longman Group Ltd — *The Hidden Persuaders*.

Introduction

This book is designed for people who wish to improve their written English. They may be in a job, like a secretary who is required to draft on her own the replies to incoming letters, or even to improve her employer's style. A man may have to prepare sets of instructions for operating a mechanism, or to set out the main points in an awkward insurance problem. Yet others may need to pass an examination in English, and among these there will be many learners of English as a second language. Some may just want to produce better writing, for the good reason that, for those whose native language it is, the 'subject' is closely bound up with personality. For instance, confused and vague writing may be the signs of a confused and vague mind; and an improvement in written work helps one to sort out and make up one's mind.

Types of English

There are various kinds of written and spoken English. The private diary, for example, can be in any style; there are no rules for it, and not many for the personal letter. But other occasions require particular styles. For instance in an examination the standard has to be adjusted to the expectations of the marker or grader. A witness's account of an accident ought to be plain and factual and carefully arranged; and a telephone conversation imposes on the speaker quite a different manner from that he would adopt for a meeting. There are as many kinds of English as there are purposes in writing, and each requires the appropriate mode of expression.

This would be daunting if it meant that the learner had to acquire skill in so many types of writing. But that is not the case; progress in one particular branch of a language is usually accompanied by all-round improvement. It is a matter of choosing the right words for the needs of the occasion; and the right choice becomes a matter of habit, like putting on the right clothes to suit the weather.

How to use   The instructional entries, like those on essays, précis, summarising, letters and comprehension can be read at leisure by those who need the help offered. Then there are substantial reference sections on the mechanics of English, such as punctuation and spelling, to which a teacher may wish to direct the attention of students with weaknesses in these departments. Other entries deal with idioms, usage, style, arrangement and reminders about grammar.

Many learners will be working on their own without a teacher. They are strongly recommended to get in touch with someone in a similar position, also seeking to improve his English, and to exchange written work. The correcting of students' work by students is a most effective method, because learners pay more attention to each other's comments than to those of a teacher. If ever you, the reader, are about to assess someone else's work, form a general impression first of all; has the writer something to say, is he interested in what he is saying, is he saying it in his own way rather than churning out what he thinks will get by? Then look at it from the point of view of the editor of a student magazine that is going to publish the piece, or from the recipient's angle if it is something in the nature of a letter; and see what improvements in presentation ought to be made. If he has any special difficulty, refer him to the relevant section of this book. If you have occasion to suggest work for someone else, or are looking for a topic for yourself, choose real tasks as far as possible: a chapter in an autobiography, a letter of thanks to anyone who has been helpful, ideas for improving the town you live in, critiques of films or TV, letters of complaint, letters to the press, an account of your chief hobby for inclusion in an opportunities directory, and so on ad lib.

Self-improvement

If you cannot find a collaborator, do some writing — perhaps from an old examination paper — and put it on one side for a week. Then do two things. First read a book that interests you; this is one of the proved routes to improvement. Then turn over the pages of this book in order to get a general idea of the contents and the assistance it offers. Look first at one of the longer sections, such as that on spelling.

Then re-read your piece aloud, or as near aloud as circumstances permit; if you can, tape it. Then consider whether it needs any correction or improvement for publication. If you are hazy about punctuation, read the section about that. Before the next piece of work read the spelling entry; you may pick up a mistake that you often make without knowing it. Concentrate on one item a week. The reading aloud will bring out any weakness; if you find yourself stumbling, look for the cause and try to find the section that will help. In any odd moment turn over a page or two of this book, and see if any of the sections specially concern you.

If you have to produce a notice, a letter, an essay or a story; if you are asked to answer comprehension questions, make notes, write a paraphrase or prepare a summary, look up the relevant section. If spelling troubles you, do not worry, because you have good chances of putting that right, but also take any hints you can find here; the same applies to punctuation and items like paragraphing and the use of capitals, ampersands, and quote marks. Look occasionally at entries dealing with questions of style. If you have difficulties with number, idioms, 'neither . . . nor', 'shall' and 'will', 'both . . . and', look them up. Should you say 'adviser' or 'advisor'? 'Standardise' or 'standardize'? It may not matter. If you are taking an examination, read the hints on the subject in good time.

Familiarise yourself with the contents of the book; keep it handy; and when in doubt about any point, look it up without delay.

Language has a life of its own and goes on its own way, little affected by the attempts of grammarians and handbook-writers to 'improve' it or influence it. It is constantly changing, adding new expressions, dropping others, and regarding as a mistake one year what will be perfectly acceptable next year. This last fact is mentioned several times in these pages, because it has come sharply to the writer that some of the grammatical forms and constructions deemed correct by the writers of various excellent guides to English are outdated and rarely used, even by educated people and the setters of examination papers. But there are still many constructions and forms of words that are generally accepted as right or wrong, especially by examiners, so I have not hesitated to use the words *right, wrong, incorrect* without arguing the case at all. Moreover some of the usages and meanings insisted on are worth preserving and the language would be poorer for the loss of them.

A

a   The indefinite article. If it occurs before a word
beginning with a vowel, like *egg*, or an
unsounded *h*, like *hour*, an *n* must be added to
make the word easier to say, thus: *an egg*,
an hour. Note that when a word begins with a *u*
sounding like a *y*, as in *uniform*, we say
a uniform. No *n* is needed because there is no
difficulty over pronunciation, as there would be
if we tried to say *a egg*, *a hour*.

abbreviations   Their purpose is to save the writer's time, by
using such shortenings as BBC and M.P. We
normally only employ them for expressions in
common use – and even then only a limited
number of agreed words like those just
mentioned, and others such as *pub*, *bus* and
phone, which have passed into the language or
are on their way there. Abbreviations are widely
used in reference books, time-tables and
technical handbooks, for example: *b. and b.*
(bed and breakfast), *h. and c.* (hot and cold),
arr. (arrive), *dep.* (depart), *vol.* (volume); and
lists of examination results consist almost
entirely of subject abbreviations. The shortened
forms *can't, don't, won't* and so on are appearing
more and more in print, but for the present it is
best to avoid them in formal writing. Where
abbreviations can and should be introduced on a
large scale are in your own notes; see
note-making.
The main groups are:

Titles and ranks: Dr, Mr, Esq., Mrs, Ms, Rev.,
St, Lt, Sgt, Supt.
University degrees, honours and decorations:
B.A., M.A., Ph.D., Q.C., C.B.E., V.C.
Time: B.C., A.D., a.m., p.m., B.S.T., G.M.T.
*Set phrases, not usually in the middle of a
piece of writing:* P.S., R.S.V.P., c.o.d., l.b.w.,
anon, N.B., P.T.O.

Places: U.S.A., U.S.S.R., Herts, Yorks., Mass., S.A.
Organisations: A.A.A., B.M.A., BR, N.S.P.C.C., N.U.M., Y.H.A.
Technical terms: m.p.h., r.p.m., oz., lb., kilo, mm, cc.

It used always to be the practice to put a stop after abbreviations, as in *e.g.*, *i.e.*, *R.N.* and so on, though abbreviations which end with the same letter as the original word, such as *Dr*, *Mr*, *Revd*, *Ltd*, have never needed one. This practice should be followed. There is also a tendency for abbreviations to lose their full stop when they are so much part of the language that the original is almost forgotten, as in BBC.
It is best to keep abbreviations and contractions to a minimum. They are a nuisance to the reader, for they slow him up — even though he may not be conscious of this — while he translates the shortened version into the full form.

-able, -ible　　Pronounciation ought to settle which of these endings is needed, but it does not always help. Try pronouncing the words to yourself, aloud if possible, stressing the *a* or *i*:

agree*able*　　comfort*able*　　incur*able*　　prob*able*

access*ible*　　aud*ible*　　ed*ible*　　elig*ible*
incred*ible*　　intellig*ible*　　leg*ible*　　neglig*ible*
respons*ible*　　vis*ible*

abstract nouns　　These are the names given to qualities and states, abstracted from the people or things or circumstances in which they are evident. For example, we think of a number of brave people, abstract or take from them what they have in common, and call it *courage*. Other abstract nouns are *beauty, cheerfulness, dignity, height, intensity*. They tend to be over-used by

politicians and men of affairs, when they speak
or write in this manner:

There is a good deal of uncertainty with
regard to the extent to which consumer
resistance was the cause of a marked reduction
in the volume of retail trade in the current year.

What the speaker meant was:

We don't know how far trade this year has
been affected by reluctant customers.

See **concrete expression; covering-up
language.**

accent
In speaking English words of more than a
single syllable, one of the syllables is always
stressed: 'All stúdents are expécted to atténd
régularly'. The tendency is for this accent to fall
on the first syllable or the syllable containing
the root meaning of the word. There are a
number of words that have the same shape as
another word, but with different meanings
according to the position of the accent. Some
examples:

cónduct, *n.*	condúct, *v.*
cónflict, *n.*	conflíct, *v.*
cóntest, *n.*	contést, *v.*
cónvert, *n.*	convért, *v.*
cónvict, *n.*	convíct, *v.*
dígest, *n.*	digést, *v.*
éscort, *n.*	escórt, *v.*
éxtract, *n.*	extráct, *v.*
fréquent, *adj.*	frequént, *v.*
íncrease, *n.*	incréase, *v.*
óbject, *n.*	objéct, *v.*
réfuse, *n.*	refúse, *v.*
súspect, *n.*	suspéct, *v.*
tránsfer, *n.*	transfér, *v.*

accusative
See **object.**

active and passive

Transitive verbs stand for actions that take effect on someone or something; and such verbs have *active* and *passive* forms:

active	*passive*
Jane *is cooking* the supper.	Vegetables *are cooked* quicker in light-weight pans.

In your own writing it is better to use the *active* than the *passive*; for example, to say 'We expect that . . .' and not 'It is expected that . . .'. The *active* is usually shorter and easier to read. *See* **transitive.**

addressing

Leave a space of at least 1½ inches (about 5 cm.) above the address on the envelope. Use house numbers rather than names where possible. Write the name of the town in capitals; add the post code.

> John Smith, Esq.,
>
> 99 Hampton Road,
>
> YORK,
>
> YO7 7BE.

See **'Mr', 'Mrs', 'Dr'.**

adjectives

These are formed in several ways. E.g. *-ful* (one *l* only) is added to a noun: *truthful*. When *-ful* is added to a word ending in *y,* the *y* becomes *i,* as in *beautiful*; Note *skill, skilful*. There are changes in the main word when *-ous* is added, thus: *fame, famous; disaster, disastrous; study, studious*. The *e* remains in *courage* to form *courageous,* showing that the *g* is soft when spoken. Most nouns can be used as adjectives without any change, e.g. *man-power, moon-dust, fire-engine, water-tank*.

The *comparative* part of an adjective is usually
formed by adding *-er* in the case of words of
one syllable, and *-est* for the superlative:
e.g. *finer*, *finest*. Note these exceptions:

good	better	best
bad	worse	worst
little	less	least

(littler and littlest are frequently used in
conversation, but at present are best avoided
in writing.)

many	more	most
much	more	most

For words of more than one syllable *more* is
normally used for the comparison, and *most* for
the superlative. Ease of saying decides any
question; there is no difficulty in saying *heavier*,
heaviest, but with a word like *probable* it is
clearly more comfortable to use the *more*, *most*
method.

There are three more points about adjectives.
Most of them cannot be used as adverbs; for
example the sentence:

You've written that beautiful

conveys its meaning, but has a grammatical
mistake that is common in the U.S.A. *Beautiful*
is used as an adverb to tell us about the writing,
but it needs to be changed into the adverb
form, *beautifully*. Similarly in 'We had a real
good meal' the word *real* must be turned into
the adverb *really*. But, as we have said so often,
language is always changing, and what are now
regarded as mistakes may be reckoned good
English in a few years.

Secondly, there are some adjectives which
cannot have degrees of comparison. For example,
a thing is either *unique*, or it is not; there is no

half-way house about it, so *very unique* is
nonsense. It is much the same with:

complete	perfect
essential	priceless
final	superior
harmless	unanimous
inferior	worthless

Finally, be sparing in the use of adjectives when
writing. Consider this:

In the blazing sunshine of Mexico, Don
clocked up an all-time record for the 400
metres, overtaking Stewart at the psychological
moment and finishing with comparative ease —
a major breakthrough for his team.

Four superfluous adjectives . . . To look at one
only; *comparative* is meaningless unless we are
told what or who provides the comparison. Five
more samples of idle adjectives, and the nouns
to which they are commonly stuck, are: *built-in
safeguard, definite decision, integral part,
necessary steps* and *true facts*. The adjectives
add nothing to the meaning, make the writing
woolly, and give the impression that the writer
is trying to be impressive. *See* **comparatively**.

adverbs   Most adverbs are formed by adding *-ly* to an
adjective: *vigorous* becomes *vigorously*. But a
number of very common adverbs have no special
endings:

before	now	already	soon	once	twice
here	there	everywhere	almost	much	
very	rather	not	quite.		

And a number of adverbs have the same form
as the parent adjective, as in these correct
expressions:

work hard   run fast   hold tight   speak slower

— though grammar books may insist that the

last example is incorrect, and that we ought to say *speak more slowly*.

Adverbs ending in-*ly* form their comparatives by *more*, and their superlatives by *most*.

In writing, place the adverb as close as possible to the word it modifies, because otherwise there may be confusion:

I *nearly* made a pound last night.
(but he did not actually make anything)
I made *nearly* a pound last night.
(but he did actually make some profit)

Again:

Even she was unmoved by such news.
She was *even* unmoved by such news.
She was unmoved, *even* by such news.

Other adverbs that need care in placing are: *almost, ever, hardly, only, scarcely. See also:* **double negatives; intensifiers; 'only'.**

Advertising   Some types of publicity debase the language by false and exaggerated usage (*absolutely unique, best on the market, save pounds by* . . .). The aim is to promote the idea that the good life consists in earning money to spend on advertised products, profitable to make. They exploit us by playing on vanity, snobbishness, sex, fear and the herd instinct. The means adopted are words and pictures; and every student of English should be able to recognise the advertising use of language; examples of it are sometimes set in examination papers.
In the language of advertisers fish and chips becomes: 'Rich golden-brown sea-food with superfine French fried potatoes as a side dish'. *See* **'like' words.**

affectation   Students who become good writers sometimes go through a period of writing affectedly. In acquiring a good vocabulary they enjoy showing off their knowledge of longish or uncommon words and phrases new to them. So that we read of *conversed* instead of *talked, demise* instead of *death*, and *dentures* instead of *false teeth*. It is an excellent thing to collect new words, but they should be kept for exactly the right occasion. *See* **clichés; dignity words**.

agreement   **1** noun and verb
The rule is clear: singular subjects have singular verbs, plural subjects have plural verbs; and when there are two or more subjects, the verb is plural.

There are some variations:

a Collective nouns: when a noun like *audience, group, council* or *team* stands for a number of people it normally has a singular verb. But, as so often, usage changes; sometimes the government of a country is regarded as singular, sometimes as plural. And when a group is envisaged as a number of individuals acting on their own it will be best to have a plural verb, as in: 'The group are going to present their opinions to the Minister'. We can imagine each member having his or her say. There is no strict rule, and it is best to go by what sounds right, as in these examples:

The crew *consists* of five experienced sailors, a doctor and a cook.
The committee *meets* regularly.

But when we think of a number of individuals behaving in different ways, the verb is plural:

The crew *have* various jobs allotted to them.
The committee *are* going to be paid their expenses.
See **collective nouns; subject, multiple**.

b The real subject. In the sentence 'A bowl of apples is seen in the picture' *is* is correct grammatically, because *bowl* (singular) is the subject of the verb. It is tempting to say ' . . . are in the picture', because the apples seem part of the subject, and they are so near the verb that they almost push it into the plural. Again, if we look for the real subject in 'Each of us has a job to do' we can see that it is *Each*; and that therefore the singular *has* is grammatically correct, even though a number of people have been mentioned. The same rule applies to *everyone* and *someone*. But the user of the book is again advised not to worry, since so many of the rules are neglected by good speakers and writers.

See **anybody, anyone**.

c Alternative subjects, linked by *or, either . . . or, neither . . . nor*, as in 'Dad or I will fix it for you'. The 'rules' about sentences of this type are broken a good deal, and we shall not try to sort them out. However one example must be given, where the grammatical rule is clear. If we say 'Neither Jill nor Jane is coming to-night' the verb is singular, because what we have really done is to compress two sentences: 'Jill is not coming . . . Jane is not coming'; and in the compressed version we think of the two separately, first one and then the other. But many people now would say 'Neither Jill nor Jane are coming to-night'; and their meaning would be perfectly clear.

d There is . . . and There are . . . Consider these sentences:

There *is* only one way of getting through.
There *are* two roads through the town.

In the first one *is* is singular, because *way* is the subject, and it is singular; in the second *roads* is a plural word, so the plural *are* is used. All these *There is/are* sentences are turned-round versions of ordinary sentences; e.g. 'Two roads there are through the town'. In order to be grammatically correct we must mentally turn round a *There* or *Here* sentence, and make sure once again what the real subject is. But it must be said that the usage in ordinary conversation is often grammatically incorrect, and the most highly educated people are heard to say sentences like 'Here's John and Mary'.

2 Fortunately for all of us who speak and learn English, it is a language without inflexions — changes at the end of words to show gender, etc. So agreement of adjective with noun does not exist in English. There are a few exceptions: the demonstratives *this* and *that* (plural: *these, those*); and a minor error occurs with one of them. In using phrases like 'This kind of transistors . . .' many people, perhaps most, are liable to say 'These kind of transistors . . .'. The reason for the mistake is clear; the mind envisages a number of transistors, and it therefore thinks that *kind* also ought to be plural; thus the singular *this* slides into the plural *these* The 'error' is much commoner than the correct version.

alibi

This Latin word means *in another place*, or *elsewhere*. It is used in English to describe the defence of an accused person who states that, at the time of the misdeed he is accused of, he was in another place. It is commonly used to mean excuse:

I've got a good *alibi* for missing the opening session, because I had to go to hospital for a check-up.

But it is best to leave the word for use on occasions when its original meaning is required.

all right   The authorities on language insist that we must
                       not write *alright* as one word, though they do
                       allow us to use *already* and *almost*. The writer of
                       this book thinks they are wrong in refusing to
                       recognise the commonly used *alright*. Moreover
                       they are depriving us of a way of distinguishing
                       between two meanings; note the difference in
                       these uses of *all* and *ready*:

                       The skis are all ready.
                       The skis are already in use.

                       – two meanings, two spellings. It would be a
                       help if we could also have two spellings for the
                       two meanings in these sentences:

                       All right, I'll see to it.
                       Your sums are all right.

                       In the first example immediately above, *all right*
                       has exactly the same meaning as *OK*, and would
                       be appropriately spelled alright. In the second
                       all right has the different meaning of *all correct*,
                       and is best spelled as two words.

alliteration   The repetition of a consonant at the beginning
                       of a number of words. It was much used in Old
                       English poetry:

                       In a summer season, when soft was the sun . . .

                       and it is found in all kinds of literature since
                       then, usually to gain effects of speed and
                       emphasis; the English language runs naturally
                       to it. Nowadays it is much employed by
                       advertisers and newspapers to make their way
                       into our minds; *Players Please, Guinness is
                       good for you* – these slogans imprint themselves
                       on our memories by means of alliteration.
                       See **doubles**.

almost   Especially in writing, place this adverb as closely
                       as possible to the word it modifies; its position

can make a great difference to the meaning of a sentence, thus:

I almost finished the job unaided.
(but he did not actually finish it):
I finished the job almost unaided.
(he did finish the job)

See **adverbs**.

alternative Strictly speaking this means one of only two choices or possibilities, as in:

The alternatives were to stay at college for another year, or to take a job immediately.

But it is now widely used in cases where there are more than two choices:

Having missed the last train home, the alternatives were to walk to Aunt Mary's, wait at the station till the first morning train, or to thumb a lift.

Probably this last usage has come to stay.

ambiguity The term applies to sentences or expressions which can carry a meaning not intended by the writer or speaker, as in this (genuine) advertisement:

Eight mongrel puppies for sale; eat anything; fond of children.

The commonest form of ambiguity is the mis-placing of clauses or words, especially pronouns; see *clauses; order; pronouns*. Cases of ambiguity usually occur when the speaker or writer is not clear in his own mind, or when in haste he uses an expression that on second thoughts he would improve:

£20,000 range for shooting enthusiasts.
The *Poet's Tongue* came out last year.

Joseph was so straight that Pharaoh made a ruler of him.

A sense of humour and a consciousness that some words have several meanings can prevent ambiguities like those immediately above. *See* **funny, unconsciously.**

American English

This differs from British English in vocabulary, small points of spelling and pronunciation. For example the Americans have kept the good old word *fall* for autumn, and they say *windshield* and *sidewalk* where we use *windscreen* and *pavement*. American slang is often vigorous and expressive (e.g. *canned* meaning *drunk*), but away from its background it can sound affected. American spelling tends to simplify, with *curb* standing for both our curb and *kerb*, the *-or* ending of such words as *behavior* (English *-iour*), and the refusal to distinguish between our *practice* and *practise*. Some varieties of American speech (which varies less from district to district than British English does) are pleasant to hear, with the open *o* and the well-rounded *r*.

among, amongst

These words mean the same. They must be used with a plural noun or pronoun, or with a noun, like *crowd*, that conveys a plural meaning.

ampersand

The sign & for *and* is best kept for one's own note-making and letters, and for titles of companies: *Lloyd & Co*. It should not be used in examinations or in formal writing.

an

This form of the indefinite article is used before words beginning with a vowel or a silent *h*, e.g. *an ice, an honour*. See *'a'*.

analogy

Note that the adjective is *analogous*, with two

a's only; and it means *similar to, on the same lines as*.

and etc.   *Et cetera* means *and other things*; thus to write the expression *and etc*. repeats the *and* unnecessarily. *See* **redundant words**.

'and' with relative pronoun
In the sentence:

She got good results from her new TV set equipped with indoor aerial and remote control and which gave excellent results

the second *and* preceding *which* is grammatically incorrect. *And* is a connecting word, but all the connecting needed is done by the relative pronoun *which*. Thus the *and* is superfluous, sounds wrong and is wrong. If you find yourself writing *and who, and which* or *and where*, make sure you are connecting two relatives, as in this correct sentence:

I revisited the River Mole, *in which* I used to fish *and where* I found freshwater crayfish.

Anglicised words
Hundreds of foreign words have been absorbed into English, and the assimilation of imported words goes on every day. The accents that words like *fete* and *eclair* used to have tend nowadays to be dropped, but it is useful to retain them in words like fiancée and resumé where they make pronunciation clear.

Anglo-Saxon   The language of the invaders from Denmark and North Germany who settled in England in the 6th century. It has provided us with words we still use for some of the most important things in life — the sun and moon, the seasons and weather, physical things, agriculture, parts of the human body and its activities. They have kept their original force and expressiveness, and are all short; the so-called four-letter words are Anglo-Saxon. *See* **four-letter words.**

antecedent   The word referred to by a later pronoun or relative pronoun. In:

The fire, which had been blazing fiercely, soon burnt itself out

fire is the antecedent of *which. See* **pronouns.**

anticipate   This word means getting in first, taking in good time the action necessitated by a foreseen event, as in:

Anticipating thundery weather, I took my mac and wellingtons.

It is too commonly misused as a dignity word instead of *expect.*

anti-climax   The descent from the sublime to the ridiculous:

The trumpets all sounded; St Peter said 'Come!' The pearly gates opened and in walked Mum.

antithesis   The contrasting of words or ideas by putting them closely together in a balanced sentence:

I know you'd rather have *tea; coffee* is ready for the others.

antonyms   The same as *opposites*; please see entry on these.

anybody, anyone
These words are singular, and any pronoun or adjective referring back to one of them should also be singular, as in these examples:

Anybody could find *his* way in a little town like that.

Has anyone a bicycle pump *he* could lend me?

or if the question were asked in a girls' school it would have to run:

Has anyone a bicycle pump *she* could lend me?

But what most people, however good their education, actually say is:

Has anyone a bicycle pump *they* could lend me?

It is grammatically incorrect, but well established by usage; and it is easy to see that anyone who makes the 'mistake' visualises a number of potential lenders and is addressing several people, and therefore quite understandably makes the subject of *could lend* plural: *they*.

Note that the words are singular, so that the *apostrophe* comes before the *s* in the possessive form:

Is this watch *anybody's*?

See **each, everybody, nobody.**

apostrophe The small raised comma used in print to indicate **1** the omission of one or more letters, and **2** possession.

1 In contractions like *it's, I'll, don't* and *can't* an apostrophe indicates where letters have been omitted. Until recently such shortenings have been considered unsuitable for business and official correspondence, but they are now beginning to appear in all but the most dignified writing, as print tries to reproduce the spoken voice. It is now pedantic to write *'flu* and *'bus* and *'phone*; but note, *o'clock, o'er.* and dialogue words like *'cos, 'bout* and *'spose*.

2 *The firm's canteen* provides an example of the apostrophe indicating possession. It comes before the *s* in the singular, after the *s* in the plural, as in *the employees' dance*.

Some exceptions to the singular rule must be mentioned, though they are unlikely to cause much trouble. In order to sound better, certain ancient names ending in *s* and a few common expressions do without the *s* that indicates possession, as in: *Moses' law, for goodness' sake*. The *s* for possession is now usually added to names ending in *s,* as in *Charles's brief case, Inverness's coat-of-arms*. If you ever have to compare the front ends of certain large quadrupeds, it is probably better to say 'The noses of hippopotamuses have no horns like the noses of rhinoceroses' than 'Hippopotamuses' noses . . .'

The possessive form of certain old words with their plural ending in *-en* is exemplified in: *men's, women's, children's, oxen's*.

It is very common nowadays for the apostrophe to be omitted in street names containing a possessive: *Princes Street, Storeys Way*. With place names there is no rule — St Albans and St Helens have no apostrophe, but the majority, including Bishop's Castle, Land's End and Lytham St Anne's, retain it. A good many plural words in common use drop the apostrophe, or appear to: *Teachers World, National Cyclists Union*.

Note that with the personal pronouns *hers, its, ours, yours, theirs* there is no apostrophe, and there is no reason for one.

apposition   The addition of a word or phrase to another word to explain it or give information about it:

William Smythe, *chairman of the committee*, adjourned the meeting.

In the next example:

The winners of the first heat — Dick and I — had a quiet day

Dick and I are nominative, because a phrase in apposition is part of the subject, in this case *The winners*. But in:

He welcomed the newcomers, *Sally and me*

me is correctly accusative because it is part of the object *newcomers*.

appropriateness

This quality is tending to replace correctness as the standard by which writing is judged; fitness for purpose is looked for rather than adherence to strict rules. Thus the question now asked of student writing is not so much 'Is this writing correct?' as 'Is it appropriate in its style? Is the student using the vocabulary and kind of expression that are right for the job in hand?' And again, 'Is his style adapted to the type of reader or audience he is writing for? Does he make things easy for the reader? Does he keep his own peculiarities in check and not inflict them too generously on his reader? Has he in general adjusted his way of writing to what the circumstances require?' Probably the net result of this change in climate is a greater tolerance on the part of examiners.

approximately

In most contexts this sounds pompous, as if it were used to add importance to something quite unimportant. Say *about* instead. *See* **dignity words**.

archaisms

These are old-fashioned words and phrases. Nowadays they are supposed to add glamour or interest: 'Northgate Primary School Summer *Fayre*'; and a hotel will hope that 'Bill of *Fayre*' will make up for high prices and dull food.

arrangement

See **material**.

as

1 This word can introduce clauses, such as:

As Jim was cleaning his bicycle, it began to rain.

As I've said elsewhere, correctness is less important nowadays.

He watched that doorway *as* a cat watches a mouse.

It can also mean the same as *because*, but in rather a weak way:

I'll pay by cheque, *as* I haven't any cash.

2 It can also introduce comparisons, such as:

My vegetables are *as* healthy *as* my father's.

When there is a negative in the comparison, it is best to use *so* in the first part:

But my roses aren't *so* vigorous *as* his.

In the example immediately above we have omitted a verb:

. . . so vigorous as his *are*.

Thus the following sentence is grammatically correct:

She is not so quick as *I*

with *I* in the nominative because it is the subject of the verb *am*, which has been dropped. But most speakers of English would say 'She is not so quick as *me*', and we can regard this as normal usage. Nowadays it is unlikely that any objection will be raised to sentences such as 'I'm as old as him'; though strictly speaking it is grammatically incorrect, and the *him* should be *he*, as the subject of the missing verb *is*.

Two cautions: *equally good as* is not accepted as standard English. Instead we must say *equally good* or *as good as*. See *equally*. Secondly, *as* must not be used as an alternative to *that* in sentences like 'I've decided that Brighton is best for our holidays this year'.

3 *As* can introduce adverbial phrases: *as before, as per schedule, as for me*. But never use *as to* where *about* will fit, for *about* is more direct and vigorous. Thus always write:

I asked *about* the patient's condition

never '. . . *as to* the patient's condition'. Similarly avoid the even feebler expression *as regards*. It makes for cloudiness; the notice 'No sugar' is translated into 'The position as regards the retail supply of sugar is currently one of extreme seriousness', when someone wishes to cover up an unpleasant fact.

assonance The repetition of similar or nearly similar vowel sounds, as in Tennyson's:

The moan of doves in immemorial elms, And murmuring of innumerable bees.

auxiliary verbs The grammarian's term for words like *will have* and *would* that help to form the tenses, etc., of other verbs, as in '*Will* you *see* him tonight?' 'I *have finished*'.

awful, awfully The adjective *awful* originally meant *inspiring awe*, and was applied to great mountains, violent thunderstorms, impressive waterfalls and so on. It is now just an intensifying word meaning *extreme, serious, very bad*, as in *awful weather, awful nuisance*. Similarly the adverb *awfully* means little more than *very*. Efforts have been made by instructors in writing to preserve the original meaning, but it looks as if their efforts have been defeated by the usages of everyday speech. *See* **intensifiers**.

ay, aye *Ay* signifies agreement and rhymes with *eye*; *aye* means *always* and rhymes with *day*.

B

back of This expression, in sentences like '*Back of* the hall is a well-equipped changing room' is not accepted as good English, and should be replaced by *behind*.

Basic English A simplified version of the language, devised by I. A. Richards and C. K. Ogden, in which a core vocabulary of 800 words is employed. It is an excellent method of transmitting clear information and giving unambiguous instructions, of getting at the meaning of verse and prose by paraphrase, and of teaching English to foreign students. It has been completely neglected.

bathos *See* **anti-climax**.

because These sentences are correct:

I'm late because my cycle chain broke.
The reason I'm late is that my cycle chain broke.

What we must not do is to mix the two and say, 'The reason I'm late is because my cycle chain broke'; this is not acceptable English. *See* **reason was**.

**beside,
besides** *Beside* is a preposition:

I do like to be *beside* the seaside.

Besides is an adverb meaning *in addition*, *as well*:

I didn't want to go out in the rain; *besides* I had work to do.

between In the phrase 'Between you and me' *between* is a preposition followed by the objective *me*. This needs to be remembered, as learners are apt to use the nominative, and say 'Between you and I'.

bi- A *biennial* plant grows for two years; a

bi-monthly periodical appears twice a month. Therefore this confusing little prefix is best avoided, even though longer expressions such as 'twice a year' have to be used instead.

blame   The correct use is shown in this example:

They blamed me for it.

Not 'They blamed it on me'.

blue-print   This word is very commonly used for dignity purposes, where *plan* or *scheme* would be better; it is best left to architects and engineers who use it with its rightful meaning of detailed drawings or design. *See* **jargon**.

both . . . and   The two words connect similar expressions or similar constructions:

She excelled both *at swimming* and *at diving*. (two nouns preceded by a preposition are connected)

She excelled at both *swimming* and *diving*. (two nouns are connected)

Those are examples of the correct use of *both . . . and*. What we are not supposed to do is to link two different items. Thus we should not say: 'She excelled both *at swimming and diving*', because we are now linking two items of different shapes – *at swimming* (preposition + noun) with *diving* (noun). It must be stated, however, that most speakers of English make this 'mistake' every day of their lives. The words are wrongly used in conversation all the time; distinguished authors are careless about them; and examiners have been known to make serious errors of this type in the papers they set. In this case 'wrong' usage rarely makes any difference to the meaning, though it could be argued that the mistakes cause writing to look untidy and inelegant.

bottle-neck   This is a good metaphor in a sentence like:

The new by-pass has solved all the problems of the Exeter bottle-neck

because the writer has recalled the difficulty encountered when a sticky liquid has to be passed through a narrow bottle-neck, and applied it to traffic. Too often however it is used in a muddled and careless way:

The new manager quietly ironed out the bottle-neck over wages.

Difficulty would be better here; there is no question of shifting anything comparable to a liquid, and in any case bottle-necks do not yield to treatment with a hot iron.

brackets   The normal kind, ( ), are used for expressions in parenthesis, i.e. spoken or written as an aside; in conversation the voice is usually dropped a little for words in parenthesis:

Jane got a pass in geography (as her teacher forecast), but failed in maths.

Square brackets, [ ], indicate something inserted and not part of the original report or message:

He told me that he had found a mus troglodytes [a rare kind of mouse] in the course of the expedition.

The rebels announced the fall of the capital this morning [in fact it had surrendered a week earlier] owing to shortage of food.

See **parenthesis**.

brevity   In writing it is normally better to use few rather than many words. In conversation we might say:

I went over to Jack Lee's house — he's a neighbour of mine — and borrowed a saw.

But it tells us no more than:

I borrowed a saw from a neighbour, Jack Lee.

Of course brevity should not be carried to extremes in normal writing. The concentrated style of telegraphese should be restricted to telegrams. For example, a journalist needing more money to buy film with prospects of some good pictures might cable to his employer on these lines:

Cashflow speediest topchances filmwise

And in pre-decimal days a boy working away from home sent a post-card:

SOS   LSD   RSVP

business English

This still persists among some writers of business letters, despite years of battering by teachers and others. It consists of writing like this made-up and slightly exaggerated example:

We beg to acknowledge your favour of 1st inst, and would acquaint you that the goods concerned (a replacement pivot) were despatched to your address per parcel post on 28th ult. We trust that your good self is now in receipt of the missing article. Should it not be to hand it is respectfully suggested that you commence enquiries at your Head Post Office.

Assuring you of our best attention at all times, we beg to remain,

Yours faithfully,

instead of like this:

Thank you for your letter of 1st May. The replacement pivot was posted to you on 28th April; and if you have not received it by now would you very kindly ask about it at your Head Post Office.

Yours faithfully,

See **letters**.

but   The commonest uses of this word are as
                   conjunction and preposition. As a conjunction it
                   is used for contrasting two statements:

                   I looked for the matches, *but* there weren't any.

                   As a preposition, it is followed by the objective
                   case:

                   Everyone finished *but me*.

but which   This expression is correctly used in:

                   He bought a car *which* had a slipping clutch,
                   but *which* was otherwise sound.

                   The *but* connects and contrasts the two *which*
                   clauses. The point is that *but* must link two
                   items of the same kind; it would be incorrect to
                   say 'He bought a car with a slipping clutch but
                   which was otherwise sound', because *but*
                   connects a phrase ('with a slipping clutch')
                   with a relative clause ('which was otherwise
                   sound').
                   See **'and' with relative pronoun**.

C

calm words   *See* **snarl words**.

can   In the sentence 'Can I come in?' the words
                   Can I mean *Am I able?* or *Have I the physical
                   power?* As the speaker is asking permission to
                   enter, it would be more accurate to say 'May
                   I come in?'. The distinction is worth making,
                   though nowadays it is being lost sight of.

can't hardly   *See* **negative, double**.

capitals   1 These are used:

                   to begin sentences,

for greetings and exclamations, like *Hullo! Good morning, Gosh!*

for the phrases that begin and end letters, such as *Dear Sir* . . . Yours faithfully (note the small f),

to begin lines of poetry, with some exceptions.

2 Capitals are also used:

for the pronoun *I* and often for the names of relatives, *Father, Mother, Uncle John*

proper names, including the names of countries and places: *Wales, Edinburgh*

titles: *Mrs* Fenton, *Lord* Smith, the *Archbishop* of York, *Prince* Philip

organisations and firms: *West Yorkshire County Council, Imperial Chemical Industries*

most terms connected with religion: *God, Buddha, the Talmud, St John, the Bible*

days of the week, names of the months, special days and times like *Christmas* and *Lent.* (The seasons — spring, summer, autumn, winter — normally have a small letter).

There is a tendency for proper names that have passed into daily currency to lose their capitals, like *bath bun, brussels sprouts, diesel engine, indian ink, puritan, venetian blind, volt, watt,* and a great many others.

case

In some languages the work done in a sentence by nouns and pronouns is shown by changes — *inflexions* — at the end of the word. But English has few inflexions; and the relationship of a word with other words in a sentence is normally shown by its position in the order:

Subject	*Verb*	*Object*
I	am reading	this book

According to their function in a sentence nouns

and pronouns are said to be in one of three cases:

Nominative:

the subject of a sentence is always in the nominative case:

Has *Jim* arrived? *He's* not here yet.

Objective:

the objective case is used for the object or indirect object of a verb, and for words that follow a preposition:

I saw *him* yesterday.

Give *her* the *tea-pot*, please (her, indirect object; *tea-pot*, direct object).

I had a nice birthday present from *her*.

That's OK by *me*.

Possessive:

to indicate ownership or connection:

Jane's bicycle

Players' entrance

woman's magazine

his turn

Nouns in English cause no difficulty, as they change only in the possessive case; see also *apostrophe, 2*. But the pronouns do change and this list of cases must be known:

Nominative	Objective	Possessive
I	me	my
you	you	your
she	her	her
he	him	his
it	it	its
we	us	our
they	them	their
who	whom	whose

In addition the nominative is used when a noun or pronoun completes a sentence:

If I were *he*, I wouldn't go in for that exam.
It was *she* who first told me about it.

The exception is *It's me;* this is now good standard English.
See **apposition; case**.

christian names

Publicity men and sports reporters started the practice, now too common, of referring to people by their christian names or forenames. This rather sickly familiarity has now spread all over the media, but it should not be imitated. Christian names are used in families, among friends and among groups of people working or playing together, but they lose their point if they are applied indiscriminately. *See* **names, christian,** for sources.

circumlocution

The term applied to round-about expressions, used to create an air of dignity and importance, such as:

In the case of cricket the school will supply equipment. (Say *'for* cricket')

From the heating point of view double glazing is *of considerable importance* to a house. (Say 'Double glazing helps to keep a house warm')

In the majority of cases essays were well written. (Say *'Most* essays . . .')

The Director of Education *is causing an investigation to be made with a view to ascertaining* . . . (Say 'is trying to find out')

See **dignity words; longwindedness**.

clause

A sentence that forms part of a larger sentence:

May I have the butter *when you've finished*, please.

I usually eat marg *because it's better for me.*

People *who are liable to heart trouble* avoid butter.

Careful punctuation or rearrangement will be needed to avoid the kind of confusion exemplified in:

At the dog show I met Joan who was showing her dog and her father. (Remedy: put *and her father* immediately after *Joan*)

Astrology is the science of writing about what might happen in a Sunday newspaper. (Remedy: put *in a Sunday newspaper* immediately after *writing*)

See **conjunctions**.

clichés   Expressions which have lost force through overwork, such as:

He *is exploring every avenue* to find a solution.

We *are leaving no stone unturned* in our efforts to discover the truth.

He is trying hard . . . We are trying hard . . . would probably be more convincing than the phrases in italics. Of course most of us employ clichés every day as labour-saving devices; there is simply not time to stop and think out exactly what we mean, and then find a suitable way of putting it. We need clichés in conversations with friends, to start a discussion or just show that we are friendly and sociable, with a few remarks about the weather or the news. But they should be avoided in writing, because they produce a tired, stale effect and suggest that the writer has really nothing to say of his own. Some examples are: *desperate killer, babbling brook, psychological moment, whispering trees, in this day and age.*

But one caution must be offered to those who

correct other people's work. There is a stage in the writing progress of nearly every learner when he uses a cliché for the first time; it is not then a cliché for him. It is a phase which has to be got through; and there are students whose first use of a cliché shows the beginnings of fluency and is therefore an occasion for rejoicing. *See* **affectation**.

clumsy expression

Here are two examples, in which the writers have not thought out what they wish to say:

When you drink anything hot you should not pour it in the saucer but drink it by the handle.

The Irish have a great love of their country from a distance.

With muddles like these, the only thing to do is to make a fresh start, even if it means writing at rather greater length, thus:

When you drink anything hot, do not pour it into your saucer; drink it from the cup, holding the latter by the handle.

When they are a long way from home, the Irish have a great love for their country.

collective nouns

Examples are: *a flock of sheep, the House of Commons, a herd of cows, the audience*. There are hundreds of them, including a large number for groups of animals: *a gaggle of geese, a string of race-horses, a litter of puppies*. The only question that arises is: should such words be followed by a singular or a plural verb? For example:

The congregation *are/is* invited to join the hymn.

There is no absolute rule; it is best for the writer to say what sounds best to him in the context. There is something of a tendency to put a singular verb after such collective nouns, though sports reporters have a fixed habit of regarding names of countries, counties and towns as plural. Thus they say: 'Manchester United *are* through to the final.'

When a collective noun is followed by the possessive case in the plural, the verb is generally pulled into the plural by the near-by plural noun, even though strictly and grammatically speaking the subject is singular, as in these examples:

A group of housewives *are* going to see their M.P.

A number of students *were* without books.

See **agreement; subject, multiple.**

colloquialisms   Expressions in very large numbers used in everyday conversation, such as *skint, haywire, flaked out, not my cup of tea.* They should not normally appear in writing; they can make it sound lazy and slapdash, and they give the impression that the writer is not troubling to adjust his style to the matter in hand, and is showing no consideration for his reader, as in this sentence from a student's examination answer:

Lady Mabeth properly mucked up Makbeth's plans.

Two colloquialisms and inconsistent spelling indicate a very casual approach. *See* **slang**.

colon   This stop (:) is used:

To introduce a long quotation or a passage of direct speech, as in:

After the Chairman had welcomed him, the minister spoke as follows:

To introduce a list of items:

Among the objects found in the suspect's car were: a saw, a torch, rubber gloves and a jemmy.

To divide a sentence into two parts without using a conjunction:

I missed the performance: I had to go to a meeting.

The authorities differ on the use of the colon; and this disagreement suggests that it is difficult to distinguish the colon from the stop with a slightly shorter pause, the semi-colon.

comma This stop is used at points at which a very brief momentary pause would be made in reading aloud. The rules about it are somewhat variable; two purposes for which it must not be used are mentioned at the end of this section. It is normally used for:

1 Clauses beginning with *who, which, when, where, if,* etc., as in:

When you've finished your essay, go on with your reading.

Practice in reading and writing will develop the sense of when, and when not to use commas with a relative clause. Note the difference between these two:

Members of the party who had anoraks did not get wet. (But some had no anoraks and did get wet).

Members of the party, who had anoraks, did not get wet. (They all had anoraks and nobody got wet).

And again:

The people on the plane who had lost their luggage went to the office. (Only some of the people had lost their luggage).

The people on the plane, who had lost their luggage, went to the office. (They had all lost their luggage).

Here is an example of how lack of a comma makes a statement nonsensical or ambiguous:

I am with-holding the address of the house where the ghost has been seen at the request of the owner.

2 Separating items in lists:

Fire equipment included a sprinkler system, self-shutting doors, smothering blankets, extinguishers and buckets of sand.

Note there is no comma before the *and* that connects the last two items. Similarly in a sequence of adjectives there is no comma between the last two:

He was always cool, calm and collected.

3 Separating words or phrases, including those in apposition:

A former Archbishop of Canterbury, *Dr Fisher*, now lives in Dorset.

Separating words or phrases in parenthesis, like brackets:

Our washing machine, *guaranteed for twelve months*, broke down in the thirteenth.

Separating words or phrases like *on the whole, however, none-the-less*:

In conclusion, I'd like to thank the Chairman for his patience.

Note that when commas act like brackets there must be two of them. Otherwise we get mistakes like this:

List of subjects, thought likely to interest

students for dissection by a committee under
Dr Price.

There are two important cautions. First, commas
must not be used to end sentences; in this
connection see *full-stop* for the quotation from a
recent report on the work of GCE candidates.
Secondly, commas must not be used to
separate two sentences, as in:

It was very wet near the Falls, sou'westers and
macs were provided.

This error could be righted by replacing the
comma with a semi-colon or a full-stop, or by
inserting *and* or *so*.

comparative adjectives
　　　See **adjectives; comparison**.

comparatively　　Use this word only when it is clear what is
being compared with what. For example, does
the sentence 'Hawfinches are comparatively
rare this year' mean that they are rare compared
with other birds? or is the comparison with
other seasons or other countries? It would be
better to say *rather rare*. In this sentence at
least there is the possibility of a comparison, but
the word is often used where there is no hint of
a real comparison, and it is inserted to add
sound and dignity. *See* **relatively**.

comparison　　Adjectives have three stages, or degrees, of
comparison:

positive　　*comparative*　　*superlative*
good　　better　　best

Very often in conversation the superlative is used
in comparing two items, but in writing the
comparative is appropriate:

Edward is the *younger* of the two.

Once again it must be admitted that most speakers would make the mistake of saying *youngest*.
See **adjectives**; **adverbs**.

compound words

Frequently in English two simple words are linked to form a new noun or adjective or verb, as in

double-decker   double-glaze   folk-tale
headstrong   makeshift   manhandle
toolshed   window-ledge

There is a tendency for the hyphen to be dropped. In pronouncing these the stress falls on the first of the two parts. *See* **hyphens**.

comprehension tests

These are supposed to measure a candidate's ability to understand his own language; they merely invite us to put into writing the kind of thing that we do mentally every day of our lives. They may include an exercise in summarising, on which there is a separate section later in this book, and a passage, usually of prose, on which a number of questions are set.

It is not worth doing many practice tests. Books of them exist, but once a candidate has worked through two or three tests and familiarised himself or herself with the kind of question set, it is a waste of time to do more. It is much better to spend the time on books of a reasonable quality and to do some fairly attentive reading.

In addition to summarising, other types of question may be asked. They involve:

extracting information about characters, their reasons for what they say and do

explaining phrases and single words

explaining figurative language and idioms

commenting on an author's style

. In answering be sure you are supplying what the question requires. If a sentence is specified, give one. If you are asked to explain briefly, be brief. If asked to provide words or phrases to replace words in the passage, supply words or phrases that will fit in, e.g. a verbal equivalent in the place of a verb, a noun or noun phrase for a noun, and so on.

For example in the three sentences below the words in italics — an adverb, a noun and a verb — have to be replaced by phrases that will explain their meaning. Suggested replacements are in brackets: note that they can be substituted for the words concerned without altering the rest of the sentence.

He accepted the post *diffidently*. (without confidence that he would do it well)

Undoubtedly the *protagonist* in 1944 was Churchill. (one who played the main part in the action)

He *anticipated* arrest by fleeing the country. (took action in advance to avoid)

See **figurative language; metaphor; simile; slang**.

A reasonable amount of time is provided for these tests. The candidate may have his or her own method of timing, but if not here is a possible scheme:

1 Skim through fairly quickly, for the general idea.

2 Read again, slowly and carefully — aloud if you are practising at home, otherwise as if aloud, shaping the words and phrases without sounding them.

3 Study the questions carefully; they are precisely worded.

4 Answer directly without wasting words. Use single words for your reply only if a single-word answer is clearly required; otherwise use complete sentences.

See **summaries**.

concord   *See* **agreement**.

concrete expression

Here is an example:

The news of the war is very bad; we are sure that in the end all will come right. — Winston Churchill

and here is the same statement muffled up in abstract words:

The *position* with regard to the war is extremely serious. We have however absolute *confidence* that eventually the *situation* will be restored.

Note, first the greater length, and secondly how the length is caused. Instead of *war* we have *position with regard to*; instead of *bad* we have *extremely serious* — and so on, so that the edge and impact of Churchill's statement are blunted. Therefore use concrete expressions if you wish your meaning to be clear. This however is just what certain speakers wish to avoid, for example in advertising, propaganda and politics. Suppose that in a country a power-seeking group has turned out the elected government by force, shot all who appeared to resist, shelled housing areas where resistance was expected, and machine-gunned people trying to escape from them. 'Peace' means that the capital is silent but for the rumble of patrolling tanks, that everything is shut up, and that bodies lie about in bloodstained streets. The usurpers would use language full of abstractions to conceal the truth:

The liberty of our people is now assured. The

military arm of our democratic government has triumphed over dissident elements, now purged from our realm by the bravery and devotion of our gallant forces. Peace now reigns in the capital.

See **abstract nouns; covering-up language**.

conjunctions　There are two main types. First, those such as *and, but, for, neither . . . nor* which link sentences of equal grammatical value:

He marched them up to the top of the hill *and* he marched them down again.

They are known as *co-ordinating conjunctions*.

Secondly, the conjunctions which introduce a clause that depends for its meaning on the main sentence:

I'll certainly come, *if you let me pay*.

These *subordinate* clauses, starting with a conjunction, are of eight kinds: time (*when, before, till,* etc.); place (*when, whence,* etc.); causal (*because,* etc.); conditional (*if, unless*); concession (*although, even if*); manner (*as, as if, as though*); purpose (*to, lest, in order that*); result (*so that, with the result that*). The terms *co-ordinate* and *subordinate*, and the names of types of subordinate clause, are included for reference, and need not be learned. *See* **clauses; correlative conjunctions**.

consonants　All the letters of the alphabet except the vowels a, e, i, o, u. Y ranks as a consonant (*York, yeoman*), but it can also act as a vowel (*happy, multiply*).

contractions　**See abbreviations**.

contrast　This device is used by most writers when it suits their needs. For example, a writer might contrast a cramped, out-of-date and battered hospital with a nearby new block of 'luxury' flats or prestige offices, spacious, warm and comfortable, in order to show the way in which spending for private profit and convenience outstrips spending on urgent public needs like medical services. Poets can condense a world of meaning into a few contrasting words:

Lilies that fester smell far worse then weeds.

April is the cruellest month.

conversation   No one teaches a child his language; no one could. He learns it on his own, by hearing other people talk, and then trying it out himself. Conversation does not stop being important; it is one of the means whereby people keep in touch with each other and stay human. It is also a means of education. The writer gets ideas and facts, learns new words and new sentence patterns. The learner-writer therefore should be ready to make his contribution to a conversation, not only as a social duty but also as a means of developing his English. Incidentally if you are stuck for a topic, try entertainment; it is a subject that everyone knows something about and probably has news about. It provides a good start because it can so readily lead on to other subjects.

correction of work

Individuals working on their own can, by exchanging with another candidate, make up for the help that they would get from a school or college; it can be a very effective method. If you are reading someone else's writing, the first thing is to get a general impression of how far the writer has supplied what the question set has asked for. If it is an imaginative composition, look for interest; freshness; sincerity; and truth to the writer's own experience. That is the most important point:

has the writer really something of his own to
say? Then you can go on to the details, which
students mark very efficiently. You can if you
like correct everything which looks like an
error, but first see if there is anything about the
composition that gets in the way of the reader's
understanding it. Writing, for example, need
not be copperplate, but is it adequate, is it
reasonably easy to read? Is there anything about
it that could be put right? Next, punctuation.
If you read the work aloud, or as if aloud, and
all goes smoothly, there is probably nothing
wrong with the punctuation; but if you stumble
or lose your way, the punctuation may be at
fault. (See *comma* especially.) Some writers
over-punctuate, and this again will emerge on
reading aloud, or nearly aloud. The use of
capitals, spelling, accuracy in handling words,
correctness of idiom and suitable vocabulary
may all need attention at different times.
When it comes to writing a letter, an explanation,
a factual description, you can be severe if
the writer is not producing exactly what is
asked for. A summary or précis should read
easily, like a piece of original writing.
Comprehension answers should be precisely
tailored to the question; see that they are not
too long. It is waste of time and earns no more
marks to write too much, e.g. by giving a phrase
or a sentence where only a single word is
needed.
If you are working entirely on your own and
can find no one to go through your papers, you
can do some useful self-correction. Put a
piece of writing aside for ten days, forget about
it, and then read it critically, as if you had never
seen it before. Again, if circumstances allow it,
reading aloud will help self-criticism; and even
more effective will be a recording on tape.

correction symbols

It is useful to have a code. Here are some suggestions:

amb	ambiguous	*Rep*	you've said this
C	clumsy		before
	expression	*sl*	slang
G	grammar wrong	*sp*	spelling
///	illegible	*V*	too many words,
MV	main verb		verbose
	needed	A *tick* for a good point
O	omit	*Underline* for
P	punctuation	something that needs
?	meaning?	attention

correctness

This quality in writing and speech has sometimes been insisted on for the wrong reasons, when dialect and deviations from official style were frowned on, as a bar to social advancement. Correctness in fairly recent times became a class badge; against this it should be recalled that for the first five hundred years of English history not more than three kings could read and write (and those uncertainly); that Elizabethan spelling was wayward and that distinguished authors (notably Scott Fitzgerald) have been weak spellers. Moreover what is 'correct' in one age is out-of-date in the next, and the slang of today may be the standard English of tomorrow. Language is always on the move.

But correctness of a kind is useful to us all, because an accepted code in matters of expression makes for ease of understanding, and the swing against correctness may have been overdone. A good standard in handwriting and the mechanics of English helps communication and avoids irritations; and we can aim at this good standard without the effort becoming an obsession. *See* **appropriateness**.

correlative conjunctions

They are: *both . . . and, either . . . or, neither . . . nor; not only . . . but also, rather . . . than, whether . . . or.* They connect alternatives and items of a similar kind, e.g. a noun and a noun, a sentence and a sentence, and (as in the example below) an adjective and an adjective, and so on:

She was *both* well qualified *and* suitably experienced for the job.

Here the correlatives link an adverb and adjective with another adverb and adjective. *See* **neither . . . nor.**

covering-up language

This is employed by governments and others when they wish to conceal or tone down something unpleasant or cruel. 'The liquidation of the Jewish problem' was how Hitler described the murder of millions of Jews. An American newspaper wrote, of one of its country's actions in Vietnam: 'One village so persistently resisted pacification that finally it was destroyed.' In our own time, when houses are destroyed to make motorways for the driving minority, we are told by well-meaning people that 'Alternative accommodation will be arranged for those persons displaced by motorway construction.' And an expression like 'Most of the poor will starve' can be made much less frightening when disguised in this way:

A considerable proportion of the lower-income groups will be liable to experience an inadequate level of nutrition.

See **abstract nouns; concrete expressions; euphemism.**

currently *Now* or *at present* is preferable.

D

dash   This punctuation mark is used for three
                      purposes:
                      To indicate a break in thought, or to add an
                      afterthought:

                      I was dreaming — can't remember what it was
                      about, though.

                      To add a summary or explanation:

                      Hooliganism, inexperienced teachers, stupidity,
                      bad buildings — all these are connected with
                      poor discipline.

                      To indicate an aside, or parenthesis:

                      Before the blast-off — which frightened me, I
                      must admit — there was much to be done.

date as postmark
                      Slovenly and inefficient; postmarks are
                      sometimes illegible, and envelopes are usually
                      thrown away. There is some justification for use
                      of the phrase when large numbers of bills have
                      to be posted.

day and age, in this
                      Nowadays is shorter and less pompous.

decided to   In students' writing the word is often applied to
                      matters of the most trivial importance that do not
                      deserve such steps as consideration and
                      decision, as in: 'We decided to have an
                      ice-cream.' The word is best kept for occasions
                      when real decisions have to be made.

definite, definitely
                      These words mean *clear*, *precisely*:

                      There was a definite change in the composition
                      of the gas.
                      It was definitely a natterjack toad.

They should not be used for emphasising or underlining:

You're *definitely* right.

'Are you coming?' 'Definitely'.

The words are also very commonly mis-spelled, with an *a* replacing the second *i*. To avoid this they should be linked mentally with *affinity*, *finish*, *finite*, *infinity*.

definition

Clearly defined subjects would make many arguments, discussions and debates more profitable. So often time and tempers are lost when two people are at cross-purposes because they attach different meanings to the same word: *behaviour, democracy, gossip, morals* and *scientific* are cases in point. For example:

Gossip about the hospital led to an official inspection.

My mother and Mrs Ross were having a good *gossip* in the kitchen.

In the first sentence *gossip* means the careless and possibly malicious spreading of rumours; in the second it means agreeable chat over matters of common interest.

Scientific method involved the careful checking of results against expectations and hypotheses.

Scientific research shows that Dentiline is 84 per cent more effective than ordinary toothpaste.

In the first sentence of the pair above *scientific* conveys the scrupulousness and honesty that we associate with true science. But in the second *scientific* has no factual content at all; it is used merely to attach the prestige of science to a toothpaste, and the sentence in which it is used has no other meaning or purpose.

demonstratives

Examples of these pointing-out words are:

adjectives:
singular — this, that
plural — these, those

adverbs:
there, then, thither, thence, here, hither, hence

A mistake, but not a very serious one, that is likely to occur is found in this example:

A member of the club said that he paid his bill only once a month. But those members should pay weekly like everyone else.

Those is plural, but it refers back to a singular noun, *member*. Demonstratives should always have the same number as the noun or nouns they refer to. Most native speakers of English make this mistake.

derivations

It would be difficult to learn the derivations of all the words we use. But it is worth remembering some of them because the knowledge often assists us to spell, pronounce, understand and use the words correctly. Especially in the sciences derivations are a help. *Atom* for instance is made up of two Greek roots meaning *not* and *cut*, so the word is used for something which cannot be split; *telecontrol* means *remote* control; and *photosynthesis* means *putting* (thesis) *together* (syn) by *light* (photo). English has the largest vocabulary of all languages; it can thus be the most expressive and if well used the most exact medium of all. The oldest English words were contributed by waves of invaders — Romans, Anglo-Saxons, Norsemen and Normans. In the sixteenth century hundreds of words came from the Continent, and since then we have acquired thousands more: from Holland, nautical terms — *skipper*, *yacht*; from Italy, words connected with music and the arts — *studio*, *solo*, *opera*; from Spain, *sherry*, *mosquito*; from the old America, *potato*, *tobacco*, *moccasin*; and from the new, *cafeteria, gangster*; and from France, *omelette, carburettor*. In addition there are hundreds of other words from other countries. *See* **words, 3**.

For those interested in the history of their language, their subject or their country the derivation of words has a great deal to offer. Etymological dictionaries deal solely with the origins of words and are full of fascinating information.

description

Students are often asked to describe something — an object, a scene, a process, the working of a device, a person's appearance or character, a state of mind or feeling. Sometimes the wording of a question makes it clear exactly what is wanted; for example the description of a power drill or spin-drier might start **1** with the purpose of the device, continue **2** with an account of its physical appearance and construction, and end **3** with an explanation of its working. If you are asked, say, for the last item only — the working of a spin-drier — you would probably omit **1**, introduce **2** only if relevant, and concentrate on **3**, with the material logically arranged. The same logical order would apply to the description of a process, such as painting a bicycle or making a pie.

There are other ways of arranging matter, in addition to the logical. There is the chronological method. This would apply to such subjects as the life cycle of a living creature, the biography of a person, a series of events, and even quite a short episode such as the breaking out of a fire and the putting it out by extinguisher or fire brigade.

Thirdly, there is visual description. This might start with a general impression, continue with some main features, and then go into more detail. Novelists describe the outward appearance of a character and then use the account as a way in to sketch the person's disposition and outlook. Other aspects of description are those of sound, smell and touch, all of which may be the major characteristic of some subjects.

The first step in writing a description is to make sure whether the question set decides the content and arrangement of the answer. If time allows, all the material that comes into the writer's head should be jotted down and then sorted out according to the arrangement suggested by the question. If a more general subject is given, for instance 'First day in a new home/school/job', it will be worth considering for a moment which of the approaches suggested above (logical, chronological, visual, etc.), or which combination of them, suits the subject best.

desirous of   Omit this expression; *wish* is more economical and less pompous.

Dewey classification

This is the scheme on which books in most libraries are arranged. There are ten main sections:

000	General	600	Useful Arts
100	Philosophy	700	Fine Arts
200	Religion	800	Literature
300	Social Science	900	Geography
400	Languages		Biography
500	Science		History

Each of these is divided into ten parts, and among the ten parts devoted to science we have, for example, 530 Physics and 580 Botany. Then there are further divisions, so that in Mathematics we have 511 Arithmetic and 512 Algebra. The process goes on till every class of book has its own place on the shelves, the books within each class as shown by its decimal number being arranged in alphabetical order of authors. Careers books are all numbered 371.425, and books on birds are labelled 598.2.

Libraries usually have charts showing the main sections, and the shelves themselves have guides giving numbers and contents; the numbering usually starts with the lowest numbers on the left as you enter. The key to the whole lot is the card index, with the aid of which you can trace any book to its place, if you know the author.

dialect

The variety of English spoken in a limited area is often a complete language within a language; it tends to be more lively and vigorous than the standard speech of the media. Dialect should never be despised, for it is a source of the sap in the tree of language. It is vivid — *stolchy*, for a sticky muddy path in Norfolk; and terse, as in the Norfolk *do*, meaning *if this happens*:

I hope it won't rain — *do*, I'll get wet through.

It is not easy to manage in writing, except by people who know it well and can reproduce it. *See* **flower names.**

dialogue

The use of direct speech adds life to narrative or description. This is how it is punctuated:

'Francis,' Mitchell said, 'have you got three boys who can walk?'
'Yes,' he answered, rather doubtfully.

'Can you walk?'

'Yes.'

'Then for God's sake go out just once more and see if you can't get some caribou!'

Note the use of commas after *Francis* and *yes*, within the quotation marks; and the commas round *Mitchell said* and he *answered*. Single inverted commas are generally used nowadays for quoting direct speech; and a quotation within a quotation has double inverted commas. *See* **quotation marks**.

dictionary

Students are strongly advised to own and use a good one. As well as telling us the pronunciation and meaning of a word, its special uses and frequently its origin, dictionaries provide a good deal of general information.

didn't ought

Ought is a single-tense word:

present:

I ought to get some new shoes.

past:

I ought not *to have bought* those cheap ones.

Note that in the second sentence the past tense is conveyed by the words in italics. It is not good English to try to put *ought* in the past by adding *didn't*. Writers who find themselves using *didn't* might try the alternative method and use *shouldn't*: 'I shouldn't have bought . . .' *See* **ought**.

different

The normal idiom is to say *different from*:

This season's fashions are very different from last year's.

But *different to* is becoming acceptable. *Different than* should be avoided, and a sentence like 'The results were different than what I'd hoped for' should be altered: 'The results were different from those I'd hoped for'.

die, dye *Die* (*died, dying*) means to leave this life. *Dye* (*dyed, dyeing*) means to colour.

dignity words These are unnecessarily long expressions, used to make speech or writing sound more important. Because they occur so frequently in student writing a number of them are listed below; the alternatives that can be used instead are in brackets:

accommodate (hold, take)
adjacent to (near)
approximately (about)
at an early date (soon)
at this moment in time (now)
concerning (about)
conspicuous by their absence (not present)
declared redundant (sacked)
discontinue (stop)
despite the fact that (although)
donate (give)
extinguish (put out)
face up to (face)
in addition (also)
in spite of the fact that (although)
locate (find, place)
made their way (went)
occasioned by (caused by)
previous to (before)
revealed (said)
seating accommodation (seats)
subsequent to (after)
succeeded in (omit as superfluous)
together with (with)
venue (place)
weather conditions (weather)
with regard to (regarding)

See also **circumlocution; clichés; padding; long windedness.**

diminutives   These are forms of words used to indicate
                    smallness, usually in friendly way. Common
                    endings are *-let*, *-ling*, *-kin*, and *-ie*: *booklet*,
                    seedling, pipkin, lassie.

direct speech   The turning of direct into indirect or reported
                    speech tests fluency and flexibility in using
                    language. Here is an example of the exercise:

Direct

'You going to the dance this evening, Sue?' asked Jane. 'I think it will be a good one – we're having the Doughboys Disco to run it, and they do a good job.'

'No, I don't expect I will,' Sue replied. 'I've got to sew up the woolly Mum knitted – and I'll watch the serial on the telly. Besides, Bob can't come; he'll be at the Tech.'

'Never mind, then,' Jane went on. 'Come next week! – and bring Bob with you. There'll be a big crowd.'

Indirect

Jane asked Sue if *she was going* to the dance *that* evening. It *was likely to be* a good one, *she thought, as they were going to have* the Doughboys Disco to run it, *because they did* a good job *of such* things. Sue replied *that she did not* expect to go; *she had* to sew up a woolly *her* Mum *had* knitted *for her*, and *she would* watch the serial on the telly. *Moreover, she added*, Bob *would not be able to go*; he *would be* busy at the Tech.

Sue *told her not to worry* and *invited her* to come *the following* week and bring Bob with *her*. There *would* be a big crowd.

Note, that generally the sense is filled out and
made more formal; conversation takes a good
deal for granted, and uses colloquial forms that

will not go into reported speech at all; and then note:

changes of tense in verbs
changes in pronouns
changes in demonstrative adjectives (e.g. *this* becomes *that*)
a direct question changed into an indirect one loses its question mark.

disinterested   This means 'having no axe to grind', 'without the kind of interest that would bring advantage to the person concerned'. It is not the same as *uninterested* (without interest). Unfortunately many 'educated' people mix them up, so that a useful pair of words for conveying quite different meanings is lost, and the language is the poorer. This is a case where it is worth trying to resist a decay in language that makes for fuzzy thinking and poor communication. For example:

Jack Roberts is very *interested* in doing the club's accounts, but he's quite *disinterested* — he doesn't get paid.

do   Note the difference between:

English   Have you got a time-table on you?
American   Do you have a time-table on you?

doctor   The abbreviation is *Dr* without a stop, because the shortened form ends with the same letter as the complete word.

double comparison
Once employed for emphasis, the usage:

Ian is *more faster* over the shorter distances

is no longer current. Note also, that words like *inferior* and *superior* which have the idea of the comparative built in cannot have the word *more* added to them.

double negative
See **negative, double.**

double past tense

This sentence is grammatically correct:

I should like *to have seen* Caesar cross the Rubicon.

But this is incorrect:

I *should have liked to have seen* Caesar cross the Rubicon

because the past tense is unnecessarily doubled: *have liked, have seen*.

doubles

These are extremely common in English, especially in conversation, and most people have a large stock of them without being conscious of the fact. They are used for emphasis, and as a short way of saying what would otherwise need more words. Examples are: *odds and ends, give and take, wear and tear, head and shoulders, hard and fast*. A number of them use alliteration: *kith and kin, might and main, safe and sound, rough and ready. See* **alliteration**.

doubt

This word is followed by the conjunctions *whether* and *if*:

I doubt *whether* he's got the necessary stamina.
He doubted *if* the news was true.

Doubt is followed by *that* only when it is negatived:

She didn't doubt that this actually happened.

See **whether**.

due to

Due is an adjective:

He hoped to get the money *due* to him.
Many accidents were *due* to icy roads.

It is widely used as a conjunction, with *to*:

Mother slipped *due to* a hole in the pavement.

Until very recently this was considered a grammatical mistake, but it now looks as if it is becoming accepted usage. However it would be better to say *owing to* or *because of* in a sentence like the last example.

duly   This is too commonly used as a dignity word; it rarely adds anything to what is being said, and is best omitted.

E

each   The word is singular and is followed by a singular verb:

Each player *has his* own locker.

Note also the position of the apostrophe-for-possession in *other's* in this example:

We accidentally took each *other's* umbrellas.

See **everybody**.

-ed, -t   The *t* instead of *-ed* is commonly used in *burnt, dreamt, knelt, spelt, spilt*. Pronunciation is not a fully reliable guide; *expressed* for example always keeps its *-ed*. *See* **-t, -ed**.

either . . . or   When these words link two pronouns in different persons the verb should agree with the second pronoun, the one nearest:

Either he or I *am* fit for the job. (verb in first person because *I* is nearest)

Either you or he *is* liable for the damage. (verb in third person because *he* is nearest)

The correct usage is rarely heard; English people normally say *are* instead of *am* or *is*. A common error is to place the words wrongly:

We shall *either* go to the ice-rink *or* the theatre.

Halfway through this sentence it sounds as if
there is to be alternative to going to the ice-rink,
such as staying at home. But the alternatives
are the ice-rink and the theatre; and the correct
version brings this out:

We shall go either to the ice-rink or the theatre.

ellipse   The omission from a sentence of words that can
be understood or supplied from the context.
Especially common are the omission of *that*
from indirect statements, and the omission of
the relative pronoun:

We thought (that) the train would make up lost
time.

The purse (which) I lost yesterday has turned
up.

Note the difference in meaning between these
examples; the words usually omitted (shown in
brackets) make the distinction quite clear:

You'll recognise John more quickly than (you'll
recognise) me.

You'll recognise John more quickly than I (will
recognise him).

enclosed please find

This is business jargon and should be replaced
by *I enclose*.

endorse   This word can mean the writing of a signature
on the back of a cheque, the recording of a
motorist's offence on his licence, and the
expression of agreement or approval.

epic   This refers to a narrative, long and usually in
verse, of the adventures of a hero. The word
has had the stuffing knocked out of it by the
media, which apply it to much smaller
happenings, such as a sporting event or a
speedy ambulance trip. Newspapers for instance

use the word in order to make unimportant events appear more important.

equally

The correct usage is:

This make of razor is *equally* good, sir.

Do not insert *as*. Also, in a sentence of this kind:

Enough is *as* good *as* a feast.

equally should not be inserted; it would be superfluous. *See* **as, 2**.

-er, or

The normal method of making up a word for the doer of an action is to add *-er*. The following words in *-er* should be remembered:

adviser conjurer (sometimes -or) promoter propeller

They are often mis-spelt because certain words for doers, especially those derived from Latin, end in *-or*, such as:

actor   author   collector   distributor conqueror   ejector   governor   sailor   tailor visor

See **spelling, 5**.

errors, common

They are dealt with under their separate headings, but are listed here because they need constant reminders.

agreement:
'At least one of the lights upstairs *need* replacing.' *Needs* because the subject *one* is singular.

apostrophe:
Some learners insert them in all plural nouns and most singular verbs: 'She goe's to classe's regularly'. The remedy is to be quite sure why and when apostrophes are added.

clumsy expression:
'I have read fifteen books which are on the back page.' They are not, though their titles are.

comma between main sentences:
'I've finished the work, I'm going out.'
Conjunction (*and, so*) or different punctuation needed.

case of pronoun:
'She'd rather go with Sue than *I*.'
Me because *with* is understood before *I*: prepositions such as *with* are followed by the objective case.

idiom:
Typical mistakes are *prefer than, anxious of*; they should be *prefer to, anxious about*. Remedy is copious practice in reading and speaking.

punctuation:
See *comma* above. Sentences are too commonly strung together by commas. The full-stop at the end of sentences is often forgotten.

sentences:
The verb is sometimes left out.

slang:
This is best avoided, except in the reproduction of direct speech.

spelling:
Many mistakes can be avoided by careful re-reading of written work.

See **mis-used words.**

essay writing   Choice of subject

Examinations tend to require two types of writing: practical (e.g. explanations, letters), and personal. For the first, see the entries *explanations, letters*. The second kind can be divided into five classes: argumentative, descriptive, factual, imaginative and narrative, but there is no sharp dividing line. The aim is to give candidates the opportunity to write about something they are really interested in, and that should help the candidate to choose his subject. Those with a special knowledge of a particular sport or hobby get their chance, but they must beware of letting a private interest run away with them; the aim must be to make the specialism interesting to the general reader. One-word subjects, such as 'Loneliness', are less commonly set now; they are harder because approach and treatment are left to the candidate; the easier topics are those which indicate what is wanted, engage the student's personality and are within the range of his or her way of life. An example is: 'You missed a holiday this year owing to illness. What holiday would you like next year, and exactly how would you plan it from the start?' This subject provides many clues; you might very briefly start with a mention of the holiday missed, to introduce next year's holiday and the detailed planning for it.

Collecting material

If you have plenty of material the rest of this paragraph is irrelevant. However if you are short of matter, jot down rapidly and briefly all the points about your subject that come into your head in three or four minutes, quite at random. If it is a concrete subject, visualise it, and that will supply ideas; if it is an abstract one, 'Courage' for instance, think of concrete examples. *See* **material**.

Arranging material

The wording of the question often decides the scheme on which you will arrange your material. Otherwise glance through your jottings, and you will probably see that it falls naturally under three of four headings. Settle on an order for the three, and put figure 1, 2 or 3 against all your items. If no arrangement suggests itself, think of possible schemes, such as: the future of . . ., the pros and cons, past and present, and the contrast they or any other viewpoints suggest, the development of . . ., the way different classes of people (e.g. town or country, young or old) regard . . ., the value or special claim to interest at present of . . ., the particular purpose or relevance to current problems of . . ., and so on.

When you have a scheme, write your essay. Do not worry about style, but say directly and simply without fuss or pretentiousness what you wish to set down.

This last – having something to say – is the key to all good writing. If you never have anything to say, acquire some interests; develop them; read about them; think how they fit in with your own and other people's lives; branch out into connected reading. All problems in learning English for any purpose are solved by practice – in reading, listening to broadcasts, conversation and writing in situations that are as close as possible to those of real life.

See **description; explanations; narrative; material: collecting, selecting, arranging; style**.

etc.

Three points to note are:

1 It is wrong to write *and etc.* because *etc.* is short for two Latin words meaning *and other things*.

2 It should be written *etc., &c*.

3 It is often used rather lazily, so that the reader is left to do the work of thinking what the other things are. It may be better instead to specify one or two more items and give the reader a clear idea of what the writer has in mind.

euphemism

The use of a name to tone down facts considered

impolite or unpleasant to mention plainly. In
U.S.A. public lavatories are sometimes called
comfort stations, while here at home workers do
not strike because the word recalls the harm
done to wives and children and perhaps to an
industry, but instead *take industrial action*. When
an employer sacks employees he *declares them
redundant*, for similar reasons. *See* **covering-up
language; dignity words**.

even

Like other adverbs this word should be placed as
close as possible to the word it is meant to bring
out or stress. Consider the difference in meaning
between:

Even she left the door open
(*She* is contrasted with other people)

She *even left* the door open
(The action is compared with other acts of the
same person)

She left *even the door open*
(One might have hoped that after leaving
everything else open she might have shut the
door).

See **adverbs**.

ever

There is a difference in meaning between

What *ever* made you do that?
(*ever* is added for emphasis)

and

Whatever you earn should be recorded.
(*Whatever* means *all that*)

In conversation the difference is brought out by
the voice. The account just given applies also to
when, where, who and *how*.

everybody, everyone, every . . .

These are normally followed by a singular
verb:

Everyone knows what happened.

But in conversation a plural verb is often heard, because the speaker thinks of more than one person; and this is accepted as good English. *See* **each, nobody, none**.

exaggeration   This is also known as *hyperbole*, and is applied to such expressions as 'He's as strong as a horse', 'I told you about it ages ago', which are common in conversation.

examination hints

The following points are obvious, but some of them are neglected every year by hundreds of candidates:

1 Spend a little time on reading and fully understanding the instructions, e.g. about length, and especially about the number of questions to be answered. Choose carefully those that really fit your particular skills or knowledge, tick them and ignore the rest. Get a general idea of the timing required; sometimes the questions advise you about this.

2 Answer the question set. Observe the minimum length if specified, but do not write too much — it only annoys the marker.

3 Number your questions and subsections if any, so as to make things easy for the examiner. Note any special instructions about this.

4 Produce your most legible writing. Any crossings out should be as neat as possible.

5 Spend any spare time on re-reading, closely and critically, for punctuation, spelling, idiom, agreement of subject and verb, consistency of tenses; you may also be able to find exacter words. Re-read as if aloud; this really does help to pick up mistakes.

examination, planning for

Get a clear idea of what is required, so that your time is spent only on what is relevant. Work out a time-table, allowing ten per cent of your forty weeks, or whatever it is, for revision; but do not be obsessed by it.

except

This word can be a verb and a preposition. Here is an example of its use as a preposition:

They all failed the test *except me.*

Note that *me* is in the objective case after a preposition. *Except* must never be used as a conjunction, as in 'Jennifer wouldn't come *except* her mother came as well.'

exclamation mark

This piece of punctuation (!) should be used sparingly. Too many of them weaken the effect. Never put two together.

exercises

For students preparing for examinations it is a waste of time to do many of these. A few can be helpful, in order to familiarise the candidate with timing and the type of question set. It is much better to do work of a kind that approaches the writing involved in real-life situations. *See* **practice**.

explanations

A process, a technical operation, a device or a piece of mechanism has to be described; and the first step as usual is to make sure what is required, and for whom. If the question or requirement permits it, the answer should start with a very brief account of the aim of the process or the appearance of the object, and then go on to give an account of its working, in logical order. Examples of items for explanation are: ball-point pen, food mixer, the human eye, a spin-drier, speedometer and vacuum flask.

F

face up to   Say *face*. *See* **redundant words**.

feeling in words Certain words do two things at once. *Fuzz* in
slang can indicate *policeman*, but as well as
pointing out a man the word also swings back
and points to the fact that the speaker dislikes
the police. This kind of language, which aims at
getting other people to accept the speaker's or
writer's prejudice, is very common in politics,
the media and everyday talk. In the three
sentences below the adjectives mean much the
same, but they also tell us about the speaker's
feeling and attitude to the person he is
addressing and the person he is talking about:

I am *firm*,

You are *obstinate*,

He is *pig-headed*.

In the sentence 'The dentist *extracted* my bad
tooth' the verb could be replaced by *pulled out,
dragged out, lugged out, yanked out* — all of
which tell us not only the fact of the extraction
but the patient's feeling about the manner in
which it was done. Here are some pairs of
words with the same factual meaning but a
different emotional charge:

outspoken	tactless
cautious	timid
reserved	taciturn
out of practice	stale
unconventional	odd
reason	excuse
willowy	scraggy
enthusiast	fanatic
easy-going	lazy
persuasive	wheedling
error	blunder

meticulous	fussy
short	dumpy
traditional	antiquated
forceful	domineering
celebrated	notorious

To be fair in argument and to keep down the temperature of a discussion it is best to use words without a load of feeling and to find a word mid-way between the extremes; between *traditional* and *antiquated* for instance stands the word *old,* and between *willowy* and *scraggy* we have the word *thin* without any colouring of approval or disapproval. *See* **'like' words; snarl words**.

female   *See* **gender**.

figurative language

This is characteristic of English and very common; it helps to drive home the meaning and gives life to the language. The commonest forms of it are found in slang, which we can regard as a large collection of words on test. All of them serve their purpose of making our conversation expressive and lively, but some of them lose their usefulness and fade away, while those that wear well pass into the permanent language. Here they tend to become so familiar that we forget their origin, as in:

I'm no *star*; I never *shone* at acting.

The two words in italics have been so long in circulation with the meanings they have here that we use them without ever thinking of the night sky or a bright light. Again, when we talk of a *fluent* speaker we are employing a figure of speech, comparing a steady output of words with the flowing of water; and if he runs short of something to say, we comment: 'He's *drying up*.'

As well as making the language of everyday life more expressive figures of speech give power and concentration to poetry:

My love is like a red red rose
   That's newly sprung in June:
My love is like the melody
   That's sweetly played in tune . . .
                    Robert Burns

Tyger, tyger, burning bright
In the forests of the night . . .
                    William Blake

figures of speech
> *See* **alliteration; exaggeration; figurative language; metaphor; simile.**

finalise
> Use *finish* or *complete* instead of this rather pompous dignity word.

finite and infinite
> Most students need not concern themselves with these grammatical terms applied to verbs. In the sentence:

> Most children *attend* school regularly

> the verb *attend* is limited by the plural subject *children* to the present tense and the plural number; it is said to be a *finite* part of the verb. The *infinite* parts are those which are not tied to a subject, such as *to attend, attending*.

floating participle
> An example:

> I saw your new clock, coming downstairs.

> This could be misunderstood. It sounds as if the clock itself were coming downstairs, because the participle *coming* is not attached to a noun or a pronoun, and is therefore said to be floating. The remedy is to recast: '. . . as I was coming downstairs'.

Punch recorded this one from a newspaper:

With the stolen car travelling at 50 m.p.h., the police again gave chase. Warning shots were fired and, *after travelling several miles at high speed*, a bullet pierced the car's rear tyre.

and commented, 'Nice shooting, officer'.

Though officially frowned on, the floating participle is usually harmless and sometimes useful. *See* **participles**.

flee, fly Parts of these verbs are liable to be confused. Note therefore:

| I flee | I was fleeing | I fled | I have fled |
| I fly | I was flying | I flew | I have flown |

flower names These include some of the most beautiful expressions in English, and they were invented by people without formal education who could not read or write, or only with difficulty. Examples are: *ladies' smocks, love-in-a-mist, enchanter's nightshade, ragged robin, hare-bell, primrose*. This is mentioned to make clear the point that there are kinds of literacy other than that tested by examinations. *See* **dialect**.

following A dignity word often used instead of *after*.

for-, fore- *Before* reminds us of the meaning of the prefix *fore*, as in *forefathers, foreman, foretold*. The prefix *for-* sometimes strengthens, sometimes has a negative effect: *forbid, forget, forlorn, forsake*.

foreign words The following from foreign languages keep their foreign plural forms:

appendix	appendices
bacillus	bacilli
basis	bases
bureau	bureaux
crisis	crises

criterion	criteria
formula	formulae
hypothesis	hypotheses
index	indices
parenthesis	parentheses
phenomenon	phenomena
terminus	termini

But the tendency is to anglicise them, and we often hear *appendixes, bureaus, criterions, formulas* and *indexes*; it seems to be only a matter of time for these and other English plurals to become standard. There is a variety of snobbery which insists on saying *croci* instead of *crocuses*; and a few years ago a well-known dictionary asked us to believe that the plural of *bandit* was *banditti*. *See* **words, 3**.

formal words   *See* **dignity words**.

four-letter words

The expression refers to Anglo-Saxon terms, among the oldest words in the language, for parts and actions of the body: guts, head, neck, nose, spew, spit. Those with a sexual reference do not occur in polite conversation. *See* **Anglo-Saxon**.

full-stop

The basic and most useful of all punctuation marks, but the most neglected; a 1975 report on the writing of teenagers notes that many of them 'have an ingrained belief that sentences end with commas, and that full stops are required only at the end of paragraphs'. It is also the easiest of stops to use properly. If you read aloud a piece of good writing by a student or anyone else you may never notice the punctuation, because the run of the sentences helps you to make the right length of pause at the appropriate points; and reading your own work aloud, or as near aloud as possible, is a good way to learn punctuation, which was devised to show pauses in speech.

The full-stop is used at the end of a sentence, and the next sentence starts with a capital letter.

It is also used with *abbreviations*; please see separate entry for this.

funny, unconsciously

Other people's unconscious humour is a warning as well as an entertainment.

As I've already told six customers this morning, we don't stock it because there's no demand for it.

Only low conversation is allowed here. (library notice)

Please excuse the circular form of this letter.

The new headmaster comes to fill a very welcome gap.

Sherlock Holmes was created by Conan Doyle who hitherto had been quite a respectable doctor.

After washing the cups please stand upside down in the sink.

See **ambiguity**.

G

gender

From a grammatical point of view English nouns do not have gender, though the third person singular form of the pronoun has masculine, feminine and neuter: *he, she, it*; and the relative pronoun has *who* (masculine and feminine) and *which* (neuter). Otherwise to talk about gender in English language is merely to introduce an unnecessary complication from inflected languages like French (with masculine and feminine) and Latin (masculine, feminine and neuter). Do not be misled by grammars which tell us that English has four genders, masculine, feminine, neuter and common; be guided by your dictionary. *See* **neuter**.

generalisations These can be too sweeping and lead to misunderstanding and ill-feeling. 'All Ruritanians are swindlers' says a tourist who thinks he was cheated out of 5p at a Ruritanian hotel; and then after an expensive bad meal at a 'luxury' restaurant a Ruritanian visitor to England comments, 'English cooking is the worst in the world'. And so on. Both speakers generalised too readily on a single case; one can hear similar examples every day of judgments being made on the basis of inadequate facts about students, parents, the police and politicians. Of course generalisations are useful; they save time; we have to make them to carry on living. But we should always have reservations at the back of our minds.

genitive *See* **possessive case**.

genteelisms *See* **dignity words; euphemism**.

gobbledygook The use in quantity of dignity words and phrases, often to make a letter sound official or impressive. This example is made up:

In general there is no obligation upon clerks on duty to supply change for any sum tendered, should circumstances arise in which a customer offers for goods or services rendered a coin or note of larger denomination than its total indebtedness, and expresses a wish to receive change. It must be borne in mind, on the other hand, that clerks have not been issued with any authority that would warrant their requesting change from a customer in the circumstances already stated.

In the genuine plain English of an actual notice:

Desk clerks are neither bound to give change, nor authorised to demand it.

See **dignity words**.

got

· This valuable utility word can make writing sound thin and poverty-stricken if used to excess; books on style have been objecting to it for two hundred years. To get rid of a few *gots* and *gets* from a passage overloaded with them improves one's writing muscles as well as the style of the piece. It is very easy to better this:

I *got* my breakfast early, but when I *got* to the office I couldn't *get* in — the lock had *got* jammed. By the time I *got* hold of a locksmith it was *getting* on, so I *got* a cup of coffee while the man was *getting* it right.

gotten

Good American for *I have got*, but less good English.

grammar

The meaning of the term has changed. It used to refer to a set of rules, drawn up by specialists, for the use of English in speech and writing; and the observance of this 'correct' grammar was for many years a sign of social status. However in this century linguistic study has shown that languages have a life of their own, devise the grammar they need, and are rarely influenced by official prescription. Thus grammar now means a description of the way a language works, and as there are several ways of regarding and explaining the complexity of a living language, there are several ideas of English grammar in circulation. However if people are to understand each other, they must observe certain conventions of speaking and writing, and the term grammar is used in this book to indicate the conventions generally accepted nowadays.

Grammatical points are dealt with throughout, but especially under:

adjectives   adverbs   conjunctions   number object   prepositions   pronouns   subject sentences   verbs

Once again we must remind readers that a theoretical knowledge of grammar counts for little, and that it is best learned by using the language, not just by reading how to use it. The grammar of English is neither difficult nor extensive. It has few inflexions and a logical word-order. *See* **order**.

great

The word is often used where a more precise adjective would be clearer. In this example the improved alternatives are in brackets:

There was *great* (widespread, deeply felt, etc.) grief in Exton when the factory was closed, but the news of a fresh light industry was a *great* (most welcome) relief. *Great* (much, extensive, etc.) unemployment had been feared, but fortunately there was no *great* (severe) cold that winter, and with the spring came a *great* (marked, considerable, decisive, etc.) improvement in the employment figures.

See **synonyms**.

group names   *See* **collective nouns**

H

had used to be . . .

Omit *had*; *used* is enough to indicate past time. *See* **used to**.

hardly

This word, like scarcely, is a near-negative, meaning *very little* or *with difficulty*:

He had hardly any money

There was hardly time to change

My cold was so bad that I could *hardly* breathe.

Hardly is not a complete negative. In the examples above, 'he' had a little money, there was just a little time but not much, and 'I' could breathe. The mistake learners make is to add a negative in order to stress the shortage or difficulty:

I could*n't hardly* breathe

If we replace *hardly* in that last example by *with difficulty*, we get

I could not breathe with difficulty

— which is nonsense. No one would want to breathe with difficulty; anyone who could not breathe at all would soon be dead. *See* **adverbs; negative, double**.

hate words   *See* **feeling in words; snarl words**.

help   Till recently this verb was always followed by the infinitive: '*Help* me *to* wash up'. The American idiom, '*help me* wash up', is now acceptable and may well become normal usage.

homely   Readers who have to talk to Americans should watch the use of this word. In England it has a pleasant meaning: *friendly, simple, unpretentious*. In America, as applied to a girl's looks, it means *very plain*.

homonyms   These are pairs of words which sound the same, but have different meanings: breakfast *cereal, serial* story; there was a *mist*, so we *missed* the boat. Do not learn lists of them; do not even look at lists of them. To do so only causes confusion where there need be none; the context in which you read or hear such words will always help. So will the linkage with related words; for examples, connect *serial* with *series*, *missed* with *miss*.

how   The word is sometimes used in an awkward
                       way:

                       She mentioned *about how* she had done well in
                       a dress-making exam.

                       Her teachers referred *to how* neat her sewing
                       was.

                       In the first example it is simpler and better to
                       use *that* instead of the italicised words, and to
                       re-cast the second thus:

                       Her teachers referred *to the neatness* of her
                       sewing.

however   With much the same meaning as *but*, this word
                       should be placed as near as possible to the
                       beginning of its sentence.

hyperbole   *See* **exaggeration**.

hyphen   This mark (-) is used to link words with words,
                       or prefixes with words: *walkie-talkie, mid-
                       Atlantic, one-third*. English tends to simplify;
                       so that when hyphenated words have been in
                       circulation for a long time they lose the hyphen,
                       as in: *farmhouse, today*. These linked pairs then
                       become single words with only one syllable
                       stressed, as in: *bánknote, lífelike, súnrise*.
                       Therefore hyphens should be kept for when they
                       are really needed:

                       1 To make words easy to say and understand:

                       co-op   head-on   lean-to   re-elect   stand-in
                       tail-less   pre-Elizabethan   anti-injection

                       2 To avoid confusion. Note the differences in:

                       a glass-stoppered bottle   a glass stoppered-bottle
                       a half roasted-chicken   a half-roasted chicken
                       an old-clothes shop   an old clothes-shop
                       re-cover   recover
                       re-creation   recreation

re-dress   redress
re-form   reform

3 In writing fractions (*three-quarters*) and compound numbers from twenty-one to ninety-nine.

See **compound words; spelling 1**.

I

i before e   *See* **spelling**.

i.e.   This is short for the Latin *id est*, means *that is*, and is used in explanations:

He invented the optophone, *i.e.* an instrument for converting light into sound.

The expression should not be confused with *e.g.* which means *for example*, from the Latin *exempli gratia*.

idea   The sentence:

She was seized with the idea *to go* to the sea

is unidiomatic, and the words in italics should be replaced by *of going*. *See* **idioms**.

idioms   These are phrases, methods of expression and shades of meaning that specially belong to a language. A young visitor to England once referred to an English friend as 'a bloody man', i.e. he was fresh-complexioned. It was a good shot at a description, and it was literally true – but it was not idiomatic. Again, 'I thought to go to the dance tonight' conveys the speaker's meaning, but the right English idiom is to say 'I thought of going'.

There are four main types of idiom in English:

1 Almost any noun, some verbs and pronouns can be used as adjectives: *football* team, *gutter* press, *winter* evening; *go*-kart, *drinking* fountain; *he*-man, *she*-dragon.

2 Grammatical errors that have become correct standard English:

It's me.

Who are you going with?

3 Metaphorical expressions such as: a dog's life, save up for a rainy day, burn the candle at both ends, bone-dry.

4 Usages with prepositions and conjunctions. There are many of these. Listed below are a few typical cases in which students are liable to go wrong, with the common error in brackets. *See* **prepositions**.

angry	I was angry *with* my friend. He was angry *at* the poor turn-out.	(angry *with* a person, *at* a thing or event; the error is to use the wrong preposition)
anxious	Mother is anxious *about* the bread supply.	(Not *of*)
between	Between you and *me*.	(Not *I*)
blame	The judge blamed the solicitor for the long delay.	(Not: blamed the long delay *on* the solicitor)
different	My time-table is different *from* yours.	(It is permissible to say *different to*, but never *different than*)
equally	Anne and Jennifer are equally good at cooking.	(Not: Anne is equally *as* good *as* Jennifer . . .)
opinion	The committee *formed* its own opinion about the plan.	(Not: The committee *made* its own opinion . . .)
outside	A detective was waiting outside the theatre.	(Not: outside *of* the theatre)

prefer	If you'd prefer a cool drink *to* coffee, just say.	(Not: *than* coffee)
reason	The reason we chose that restaurant is *that* we've never been kept waiting.	(Not: . . . is *because* we've never been kept waiting)
same	The model you got from the shop is the same *as* the one I bought in York.	(Not: the same *which* I bought in York)
substitute	We'll have to substitute marg *for* butter.	(Not: *by* butter)
superior	We find unbranded lines superior *to* advertised stuff.	(Not: superior *than*)
up	The firm *kept up* the quality and reputation of their goods for many years.	(It is unwise to leave the word *up* till late in the sentence, i.e. after *goods*)

In addition, certain words are rarely used in the plural; *advice, assistance, co-operation* and *information* are examples.

if   *See* **whether, if**.

imperative   The name given to that part of a verb which is used for a command: *Halt! Cheer up! Go slow!*

impersonal constructions
Examples are:

It appears that . . .

It was said that . . .

It looked as if . . .

The next step was to . . .

Such expressions are useful when a writer

wishes to keep himself and his opinions out of
his writing; as for example a civil servant is
required to do when he is sending an official
letter. In quantity such impersonality makes for
rather dull and colourless writing. Another place
for impersonal writing is in the setting out of
instructions for the use of a device or kit. Here
the writer will be anxious not to be too
assertive, and will avoid such phrases as 'You
must now . . .' Instead he will write in this
style:

Lubrication is effected by removing the circular
black cap on the gear-box. Sufficient grease
should then be inserted until the box is two-
thirds full. The cap should be replaced tightly.

See **one**.

imply, infer   These words have different meanings, but they
are often confused. To keep them distinct is an
aid to clearer expression. *Imply* means *strongly
suggest*:

He implied that he was a member of the club,
without ever asserting it.

Infer means *to gather* or *learn*.

And those present inferred from his
knowledgeable conversation that he was in
fact one of them.

in-, un-   There is no rule for deciding which of these
prefixes should be used to negative a word. On
the whole, words that come from Latin or
French have *in-*: *impossible, irresponsible,
indirect*; and words of Old English origin have
un-, as in *unhurt, undying, unwilling*. But there
are many exceptions, and as usual practice
makes perfect. *See also* **un-, in-**.

indirect speech Sometimes known as *reported speech*. *See*
direct speech.

individual This word is often used rather loosely to mean just a *man*, a *person, somebody*. It is probably best to keep it for use in cases in which an individual is being contrasted with a group or crowd:

Ford's first cars were all black; he did not cater for individual tastes.

infinitive *See* **finite** and **infinite**.

inflated English The use of too many words produces this. For example 'He voiced the opinion . . .' is a blown-up version of *said*; and instead of telling a civil servant to buy a book a government department wrote:

You are authorised to acquire the work in question by purchase through the ordinary trade channels.

See **gobbledygook**; **dignity words**.

innuendo A suggestion that is hinted, but not expressed outright. Here is an example from an exchange of words between a judge and a barrister in a court of law:

Barrister: Now if I saw your lordship going into a public house . . .

Judge: 'Coming *into* a public house' I think you mean, Mr Smith.

inside The correct usage is: 'There was a seat inside the shelter'. The common mistake is to say *inside of*.

insinuation *See* **innuendo**.

intensifiers The term sometimes used for words that strengthen the meaning of other words:

*serious*ly ill (strenthens an adjective)
very hurriedly (strengthens an adverb)

a *substantial* increase (strengthens a noun)
rinse *thoroughly* (strengthens a verb)

Used sparingly, such intensifying adjectives and adverbs can add muscle to what is being said. But like muscles, they can be weakened by being overworked without rest; and they are often overstretched in this way by people who wish to stress points and make out a strong case. For example, a broadcaster on road conditions might say:

In this month's weather a *substantial proportion* of winter nights are *undoubtedly* going to be *decidedly* foggy and frosty, with the result that *an appreciable number* of motorists will *definitely* be in *very real* danger of a serious accident.

This would probably have more effect on the hearer if it read thus:

Winter nights are liable to frost and fog, and many motorists will risk accidents.

Some of the intensifying adverbs that should be used sparingly in writing are:

appreciably   completely   considerably
definitely   literally   perfectly   practically
really   simply   terribly   truly   very

interjections   These are single words usually, like *hallo! right! gosh!* Such expressions as *shut up, go away*, are not interjections, but complete sentences. *See* **exclamation mark**.

interviews   Facility in the use of appropriate English can be a great help to candidates for jobs or places in educational institutions. An example of how not to respond is provided by the candidate for university entry who was asked if he read much. He replied, 'Ah'm not fussy' — in other words he showed no discrimination in his reading, and implied that it did not matter to him what he read. This was unwise. Not only did he reveal a weakness, but he made the mistake of using the wrong vocabulary; 'fussy' in this context is altogether too chatty a word.

Interviewers are normally anxious to give the people they are seeing every opportunity to show themselves at their best. Interviewees can help themselves by thinking in advance of the likely questions and the appropriate answers; by answering fully — not just *yes*, but *yes, because* . . . and so on; and by using rather more formal language (e.g. no slang) than that spoken in everyday conversation. The selectors may ask candidates to give information which has already been supplied on an entry form. This is not stupidity on their part, but merely their wish to hear the candidate speak up for himself.

intransitive *See* **transitive**.

inverted commas
See **quotation marks**.

irony The word describes

1 a particular use of words and

2 special situations in films, plays and real life. In the first, a person chooses words in speech or writing to convey a meaning opposite to that of the words. Imagine that in a certain country a group of politicians or soldiers seizes power by force and sets up what it calls 'a people's democracy', applying any and every method to make themselves secure. The reporter for a British paper describes the process for us:

These *upholders of democracy* and *people's rights* have imposed a curfew, forbidden public meetings, censored the media and muzzled the press, besides setting up concentration camps for such of their opponents as have not escaped from *this paradise on earth.*

Clearly the reporter thinks the usurpers are anything but democrats and their régime a repressive and cruel one; and he exposes their claims by attaching their fine 'democratic' labels to the facts of suppression. Similarly with *paradise*; he reminds his readers that conditions are anything but paradisal by saying that they *are*, thus stimulating an immediate denial in the minds of those readers.

The second kind is *dramatic irony*. Here (for example) one of the characters in a play says things with a double meaning that is fully understood only by the audience. In Shakespeare's *Macbeth*, Duncan, a popular and successful king of Scotland, is about to visit one of his generals — Macbeth himself. The latter and his wife plan to murder Duncan on this visit and then to seize the throne. In the scene just before the arrival of Duncan to put up for the night, Lady Macbeth says:

He that comes must be provided for . . .

The audience, but not the characters, understand the real meaning ('We must kill him') that lies under her politeness.

-ise, -ize   Should words like *standardise, criticise* end in *-ise* or *-ize*? Americans tend to use *-ize*, but we recommend the use of *-ise* as a general rule, because there are some words like *surmise, exercise* that must have an *s*. But all the *-ize* words can be spelled *-ise*. *See* **spelling, 1**.

italics   There are three uses of these sloping letters:

1   For titles of books, plays and films.

2   Occasionally for emphasis, to bring out a word

that would be stressed in conversation. They should be sparingly used for this purpose.

3 For imported foreign words.

It is worth noting that when material, such as a programme, is sent to a printer any words that need to be set in italics should be under-lined.

its, it's   *Its* is the possessive case of *it*:

The dog can't find *its* bone.

It's is short for *it is*;

It's buried in the garden.

Keep them separate by remembering that *it's* is an abbreviation, just as *it'll* is short for *it will*.

J

jargon   Groups of specialists like civil servants, scientists, business men, critics and craftsmen develop a language of their own for use on the job and in conversation with their fellows. Such a language is their jargon, and if they use it in ordinary speech or writing confusion can be caused, because outsiders cannot be expected to know what they are talking about. Also ordinary people sometimes use jargon, because it sounds impressive or clever, and bring in roundabout expressions and unnecessarily long words. For example we read about 'prowess in the field of academic achievement' instead of 'academic success'. Here is a selection, from politics, medicine and the civil service, of jargon words that are best left alone — except when using *allergic, ceiling, overall, phobia, redundant* and *target* in their literal sense:

accommodation unit (for dwelling)   allergic
bottleneck   breakthrough   ceiling   escalation

finalise   global   medical adviser (for doctor)
overall   phobia   redundant   target

See **technical terms.**

journalism

Newspapers exist by turning out a regular supply of arresting news. However exciting events do not happen often enough to provide morning and evening headlines, so a special monosyllabic language has been evolved to make small news seem big. This jabbing shorthand includes words never used in real life with their journalistic meaning:

ban   bid   blast   boost   claim   crack   dash
grim   king ('oil king')   lash out   pact
probe   quit   quiz   rap   rush   shock   slash
soar   top

For example, a bishop might suggest that it would be tactless to supply wine or beer at a lunch to which Arabs were invited, because Muslims are forbidden to drink alcohol. This small piece of tact would be blown up thus:

Bishop's Beer Ban Bid

Further examples: Show Biz Pay Slash Shock; Police Probe Oil Kings Pep Pact; Rogue M.P. Raps British Bread. *See* **alliteration.**

K

kind

It is correct English to say:

This kind of transistors needs an aerial

but in conversation we often say:

These kind of transistors need an aerial.

We think of many examples of one type, and so put *these* in the plural, forgetting that the word *kind* is singular. In written English it is best to avoid the error if possible. *See* **agreement, 2.**

L

language, changes in

A living speech is constantly trying out new words and expressions, and borrowing from other languages. As new interests, propaganda, and new modes of living assert themselves, the vocabulary changes. Space travel, advances in medicine, popular travel, fashions in dress and eating and the use of leisure all introduce new terms. *Disc jockey, radar, lay-by* are all established, but other expressions have yet to make their way.

latter

The correct usage is:

Both Daphne and Joan were invited, but only the latter could come.

That is, the word refers back to the second of two items just mentioned, and in the above example the word *latter* avoids the repetition of *Joan.* It is best not to use it in any other way.

lay, lie

The transitive verb 'to lay' must have an object:

The battery hen lays dull eggs.

It is liable to be confused with the intransitive verb *to lie*, because one of their forms is common to both: *lay*. The following should be learnt:

She lays the table	She lies down
She was laying the table	She was lying down
She has laid the table	She has lain down
She laid the table	She lay down.

Laid is sometimes spelt wrong; remember it by its family: *paid, said, afraid*.

legal language

This is the style employed by lawyers in drawing up contracts, wills, laws and official regulations. There has to be no doubt about the meaning in such documents, otherwise people might twist the will, evade their obligations or find a way to get round a rule. This legal language can be long-winded, repetitious and cumbersome; and there will be *aforesaids* and *theretos* to make quite sure what is being referred to. Legal language should be left to lawyers and not borrowed to add a dignity to one's own writing.

less   Keep *less* for quantities:

The new timetable allows *less* time for changing buses.

Decimalisation meant *less* chocolate for the same money.

Use *fewer* for number:

Fewer trains mean more road accidents.

We see *fewer* birds now the trees have gone.

letter writing   The advice that follows applies to all types of letter; recommendations for particular styles are given in the next entry.

The full address should be written at the top right-hand corner of the page, with the date (not the day of the week) below; if there is a telephone number it should go in the top left-hand corner. There is no need for any punctuation in the address. All these items should be reasonably spaced. If you look at the open pages of this book you will see that the print is framed by a white margin all round; letters have a similar margin.

Capital letters should be used for all words of the opening, thus:

Dear Mr Smith
In the closing phrase only the first word,
Yours . . .

needs a capital. The signature should be roughly parallel with the lines of writing, and be legible; people who have difficulty in writing their names clearly should type or write them in capitals below the signature.

In all letters the principle of good writing applies: the style should be suited to the occasion.

On the envelope there should be a space of at least $1\frac{1}{2}$ inches above the address so that it is clear of the post-mark. Use numbers of houses where possible rather than names; put the name of the post town in capitals, followed by the county name in full, unless it has an accepted abbreviation, such as *Lancs.*; add the post code below. It is a good idea to put your address on the back of the envelope, so that if it goes astray it will be returned unopened. *See* **addressing**.

letters, style of: opening, close, contents

The ways of beginning and ending a letter vary according to its purpose and the relationship between the sender and receiver. There are three main types:

1 Business and official letters, for example between an individual and a firm supplying goods, or between a government department and a member of the public. This type starts:

Dear Sir *or* Dear Sirs *or* Dear Madam

— the middle one will not often be needed — and ends

Yours faithfully . . .

The style here will be cool and show no friendliness, because the people corresponding do not know each other and probably never will. When you reply to a business or official letter always quote the reference given; this will ensure that your answer reaches the right office in an organisation which may have scores of branches and thousands of employees. The content of the letter should be brief and relevant, keeping strictly to the matter in hand. The style should avoid slang and chattiness on the one hand and business jargon on the other. By 'business jargon' (now avoided by good firms) is meant by writing of this kind:

Yours of the 5th inst to hand. In reply we would intimate that when our Mr Robson called at your residence on the 29th ult . . .

What should have been said is:

Thank you for your letter of June 5th. When our representative called on May 29th . . .

See **business English**.

If you receive an impolite letter, do not reply in the same way; rudeness in a letter should always be avoided. The most telling reply is to be polite. It you have occasion to complain, a reasonable letter is always the best move towards getting things put right. In short, whether a business or a government department is concerned, time is saved and irritation avoided by letters which are clear without being brusque, polite without being smarmy, and firm without being rude or domineering.

2 Less formal letters between people who know each other a little without being close friends. These start:

Dear Mr *or* Dear Mrs *or* Dear Miss *or* Dear Ms *or* Dear Dr

and end

Yours sincerely

The content will be matters of interest to both, the purpose may be to keep up or develop a friendship or just to make an appointment for a 'flu injection; the style will be relaxed and informal.

3 Completely informal letters between close friends or relatives start 'Dear Joan' or in other ways; they have endings such as 'Yours ever', 'With love to you all' and so on.

There are variations such as 'Yours truly' and 'Yours very sincerely' and in very informal letters such expressions as 'Yours till hell freezes'. But on the whole endings like the last should be avoided, because what is bright and amusing when said on the spur of the moment can seem very dead when written down.

In recent years there has come from America a tendency for formal letters of Type 1 to begin and end in the style of Type 2. This may have been due sometimes to commercial reasons; a firm like a mail-order house that exists by persuading people to part with money by appearing friendly and helpful, will adopt an informal manner to get on good terms with its customers, and thus sell more of its wares. In governmental letters too there has been a trend towards greater friendliness, to show the recipient of an official letter that she or he is regarded as a human being, and not just as a number in a file. Letters from civil servants used to start 'Sir' or 'Madam' and end 'I am, Sir, your obedient servant', but nowadays, unless there is a special reason for coolness, they write 'Dear Mr' and end 'Yours sincerely'.

Thus the way a letter is written is decided by its purpose and the relationship between sender and receiver; so think of your reader all the time you are writing one. For example, letters between a student and the principal of his college should never use the 'Dear Sir' approach; it is much too stiff for a message between people who are supposed to know each other. Again if a pupil or recent pupil at school writes to someone on the staff for a testimonial, she or he should employ the 'Dear Mr . . . Yours sincerely' style. The fact that something is being asked for shows a degree of acquaintance and perhaps friendliness that debars strict formality; it is positively unhelpful to use a cold informal manner in such cases.

licence, license

You get a new *licence* (noun with a *c*) but you *license* (verb with an *s*) a car. The two get a good deal confused, and it does not greatly matter. Remember the difference by *advice* (noun) and *advise* (verb), where the pronunciation settles it.

like

This adjective ('He's like his mother') is very often used as a conjunction in conversational English:

If you write *like* I do, you'll fail!

Standard English would correctly use *as*:

If you write *as* I do . . .

At present it is advisable to use *as* in such sentences in written work.

'like' words

These tell us more about the user's feelings and the way he wants us to feel than about the subject mentioned. In the sentence:

There's an *old-fashioned* stone sink in the kitchen

we are given information; the sink is probably about forty years old. But if a shop tries to sell us 'Old-fashioned Hot Cross Buns' the term *old-fashioned* contains no factual information whatsoever, and tells us nothing at all about the buns. They are newly made, according to a modern recipe, by up-to-date methods in a modern bakery, etc. But the vendor wants us to *feel* that they are made of good old-fashioned materials with unmodern individual care according to a traditional recipe; if he can make us feel that way his hand is halfway into our purse. *See* **feeling in words; snarl words**.

literally

The adverb of *literal* means *according to the letter, taking things in their usual and obvious sense*. Thus:

The refugees were *literally* starving

means that they were likely to die unless fed. However the adverb is often wrongly used to strengthen and intensify a speaker's meaning:

My heart literally jumped into my mouth when the bus skidded.

Delilah's singing literally brought the house down.

loan

This is a noun; the verb is *lend*. Thus *Lend me an umbrella* is correct — not *loan me*.

longwindedness

This has been mentioned under other headings, but it is necessary to insist once again that too many words for the purpose just obscure the meaning and irritate the reader:

On reaching *my residence* (home) I was *greatly concerned* (worried) by *observing* (seeing) black smoke *in the vicinity of* (near) the back door, *to which I endeavoured to gain access* (which I tried to enter).

See **circumlocution**.

lot of

This and *lots of* have come to be regarded as adjectives. So that it is correct to say:

A lot of people *have* entered for the cross-country

because it is the people (plural) who have entered. *See* **collective nouns**.

loud

This can have two adverbs, *loud* and *loudly*, one for short expressions in everyday speech:

You're playing your trannie too *loud*

and *loudly* for other uses:

The gears protested loudly when mishandled.

See **adverbs**.

M

main verb

Dickens' novel *Bleak House* starts with a whole page without a main verb. He is describing a London fog which blankets the sight and thwarts all movement, and he uses nouns and adjectives to convey the sense of deadness:

For everywhere. Fog up the river, where it flows among green aits and meadows; fog down the river, where it rolls defiled among the tiers of shipping, and the waterside pollutions of a great and dirty city.

But examination candidates should see that all their sentences have main verbs. *See* **sentences**.

mainly

This adverb, like *only*, should be placed next to the word it modifies. Note the difference between these two:

That afternoon she mainly washed the floor for her mother.

That afternoon she washed the floor mainly for her mother.

See **adverbs**.

majority

This tends to be used as a dignity word where *most* would be better; and it should in any case

be used only for number and not for quantity.
It is correct to say:

The *majority* of householders like a garden.

But 'The *majority* of his garden is covered with weeds' is incorrect.

malapropism   The word applied to a ludicrous mistake made by a person who tries to use long impressive words and gets them comically wrong.
Once I heard a man say 'I can't *domesticate* my food properly till I get my new teeth'; and a cleaner is reported as saying 'I've to *consecrate* on Mr Smith's room this morning'. But not all such mistakes should be laughed at; they may just show a respect for education on the part of people who wish they had had more of it.

material: collecting, selecting, arranging
You may have all the matter needed for writing an essay ready in your head, or you may be stuck for material. If your subject does not suggest ideas at once, try visualising; for example if you are given the abstract word 'Loneliness', visualise people in lonely situations – men in a lighthouse, women alone in the house all day, children in a big new school, workers in a vast factory, and other obvious examples. You may find that they fall into two classes, such as physical loneliness and mental loneliness. Again, you can just ask the 'wh' questions: who, what, why, when, whither, whether, where. Or employ the free association method: jot down any and every point about the subject that comes into your head, however trivial some of them seem. One will lead rapidly on to another; about twenty will be a good start.

The selection of material will depend on your approach to the topic, and this approach will often be decided by the way the question is set.

The longer the subject in the exam paper, the easier it will be to answer, because in this way the examiner provides candidates with ideas for arrangement, such as 'pro-and-con' or 'past-present-and-future'.

The points jotted down should be sorted out under two or three main headings; others that do not fit in may provide a beginning or a conclusion. It often happens that a glance at the list of points suggests a good arrangement. A capital A should be put against points suitable for an opening, B, C and D for the main paragraphs, and E for those that will help to form a conclusion. It is advisable not to have too tight a scheme; it would take up too much time. When there seems to be enough material for the paragraphs, start writing; fresh points will occur as you go along.

It is helpful to write skeleton essays: that is, to jot down material on a particular subject, and then to sort it out and arrange it in note form. If possible the opening and concluding paragraphs should be written in full. This is an excellent exercise in assembling material and mobilising the mind, and it is specially useful if time is short.

See **essay writing**.

mathematics If the *e* is pronounced the spelling will not slip. The word is singular when it means a branch of learning:

Mathematics *is* her best subject,

but plural when it refers to calculations:

If the bank's mathematics *are* correct, I'm hard up.

may, might Examples of the difference:

She *may* break the record (i.e. it is quite possible).

She *might* break the record (i.e. it is just possible, but not very likely).

metaphors   Two examples of one metaphor:

Grammar schools are said to have *creamed off* the most able children (i.e. they are said to have taken the most able children, like someone taking the cream off the top of the milk).

You're *the cream* in my coffee (i.e. you're the finishing touch of perfection for me, just as cream makes a cup of coffee perfect).

Note how long and cumbersome are the explanations of each of the metaphorical expressions. The aim in using metaphor is always to pack in the maximum meaning by describing one thing in terms of another:

The group's latest number *rocketed* to the top of the table.

A group of pop singers is not a rocket, but its sudden rise to popularity is illustrated by comparing it to the speed of a rocket. English is full of metaphors: wages *axed*; prime minister *hits* back; prisoner's *bid* for freedom; *star* turn; a *dog's life*; the *penny dropped* at last; a *web* of deceit; a *flood* of complaints. Newspapers love metaphors, and sometimes get very muddled in using them:

Homes *target* hits *ceiling*.

mid-atlantic   A form of language used solely on the media, never in real life, in which the speaker puts on a semi-American accent. It is favoured by sports casters and TV advertising.

minority   Too frequently *a minority of* (6 syllables) is used as a dignity expression for *few* (1 syllable).

**mis-used
words**   There are many of these; they lose a clear

meaning through mis-use, as a chisel used as a screwdriver loses its edge. Examples are:

alibi means 'in another place'. It is not a synonym for *excuse*.

anticipate means 'to take action early, in good time' as in 'He anticipated the coffee price rise by purchasing a hundredweight of it'. It does not mean *expect*.

infer means 'deduce' or 'conclude'. It is not an alternative to *imply*, which means 'suggest'.

while means 'during the time that':

While I was cutting bread two wasps got into the jam.

It also shifts its meaning a little to mean *although* in some sentences:

While his father did not expect brilliant results, he did want his son to work hard.

See **errors, common; vogue words; 'while'.**

'moment in time, at this'

Does this expression mean more than *now*?

more

This must not be used with words like *unique, inferior, superior, preferable*, because each of these words already includes the idea of comparison. For example, a thing is either unique or it is not; for though it is reasonable to say *nearly unique*, it is absurd to say *more unique*. Similarly with *superior* and *inferior*; they already have the comparative *more* or *less* built into them. Again, *preferable* already means *more-to-be-chosen, better-to-choose-this-one*. *See* **adjectives.**

most

It is good American to say:

Most all people present enjoyed the singing.
Most everyone put a coin in the plate.

But it is not current English, and to use *most* in this way makes the speaker sound as if he were putting on an affectation of being American.

Mr, Mrs, Dr   No full stop is needed after these abbreviations, because the shortened form in each case ends with the same letter as the complete word. Note that *Mr* and *Dr* are not used with *Esq.*, so that we write on an envelope *either*

Mr John Smith
or
John Smith, Esq.

Esq. is thought to be more dignified than plain *Mr. Ms* is coming into use as a written term of address for women; it does not indicate whether the person addressed is married or not. *See* **abbreviations**.

multiple choice questions

These are set by some examining bodies, as part of a comprehension test. The candidate is asked to read a passage of prose and then to answer a series of questions. A point in the passage – the meaning of a word or a phrase, the drift of a paragraph, the significance of a particular expression – is selected; and five or so answers are presented, of which only one is correct. The candidate is then required to indicate which he thinks is the right answer by ticking or blocking one of the spaces next to the suggested answers. Here is an example:

Question 3
The word *myriad* in line 3 means:

minute   ☐
innumerable   ☐
shining   ☐
abundant   ☐
perfumed   ☐

A multiple choice comprehension test will consist of up to twenty-five such sets of suggested answers. Apart from doing a practice paper, no special preparation is needed for these tests, and there is no point in working through a number of them.

multiple subject

See **subject, multiple**.

N

names, christian

Also known as forenames, these come from the Old Testament (e.g. David), the apostles and others in the New Testament (John), saints and martyrs of the Christian Church (Cecilia, Bernard), and heroes and heroines of myths and legends and history (Helen, Arthur, Harold, Florence). For misplaced use, *see* **christian names**.

narrative

The first step in writing narrative is to decide what events and other material you are going to put in. There may be good reasons for skimping a dull series of events and giving more space to an important episode. It may also be necessary to look at things from more than one point of view. Shakespeare did this in the last act of *Macbeth*, where the action takes place alternately inside the castle with the besieged murderer, and outside with the besiegers, till they both meet in the final scene. The same tense will have to be used throughout, the present being introduced in dialogue at dramatic moments; direct speech enlivens a story and keeps it going. *See* **dialogue; time**.

negative, double

This is an example of the acceptable use of a double negative:

The reflecting studs in the middle of the road are called catseyes because they are *not unlike* the eyes of a cat.

The two negatives make a plus: 'the studs are *rather like* the eyes of a cat'; and they provide a shade of meaning different from that of the plain *like*.

Otherwise double negatives must be avoided, though they used to be brought in for emphasis by distinguished writers. These are examples of the kind which is not permissible, with the correct usage in brackets:

I don't want *none* (any) of your nonsense.

They never caught *no* (any) fish in that river.

He hadn't *never* (ever) been to London.

And a reminder that certain near-negatives, like *hardly* and *scarcely*, must not be negatived:

I *don't* hardly ever go home at weekends now. (Omit *don't*)

They had*n't* scarcely time to catch the bus. (Omit *not* in *hadn't*)

See **hardly; scarcely**.

neither

In English the word rhymes with *scyther*; in America it is pronounced *neether*.

neither . . . nor

With this pair of correlatives it is important to get *neither* in its right place:

I have *neither* the time *nor* the inclination to play golf.

The words *the time* are being negatived, so the negative *neither* goes closely with them. The mistake often made here is to say

I neither have the time nor the inclination . . .

which is wrong because it removes *neither* from
the words which it correlates with *inclination*.

The words *neither . . . nor* are normally followed
by a singular verb, because in the sentence

Neither Sheila nor Mary *was* able to come

the two girls are thought of separately. However
it is extremely common among people who
speak good English to say *were* in a sentence
like this. *See* **correlative conjunctions**.

neuter

Nouns in English grammar have no gender, and
this is not altered by the fact that certain words
like *actress, vixen, mistress* are used to denote
the sex of the person or animal referred to. It is
merely confusing to introduce the terms
masculine, feminine and *neuter* into English
grammar, when there are only a couple of
pronouns – *it* and *which* – that can be regarded
as neuter. *See* **gender**.

never

It is sometimes used as a substitute for *not*:

'Did you borrow my bike?' 'I never . . .'

This usage is briefer and a little more emphatic
than the correct I *didn't*, but it is best avoided as
it can lead to ambiguity.

**nobody,
no one**

The words are singular:

There was no one on the terraces.
Nobody *wants* to lose his pay.

See **everybody**.

nominative

The subject of a verb must always be in the
nominative case, as with these pronouns:

Jill and *I* (not *me*) and a lot of others went to the disco.

Brian and she (not *her*) came to the meeting early.

See **case; subject.**

none This is usually singular and followed by a singular verb:

We invited three people, but none *has* replied.

None of my friends *is* on the phone.

None of the food *is* appetising.

But it is often used in conjunction with a plural word, and followed by a plural verb, as in this example:

None of the competitors *were* ready.

The writer can go by instinct; and if his instinct is wrong, it matters very little as in this case. *See* **everybody.**

not only . . . but also

Normally *not only* is followed by the complete *but also.* However it is quite permissible to omit the *also*, if it sounds right to do so:

He not only promised to repair the roof, but came the same day.

Like other correlatives the *not only* should be placed as close as possible to the first of the words or phrases it correlates, as in:

They brought *not only their guitars*, but also a lot of music.

The common error is to place the *not only* in between *They* and *brought. See* **correlative conjunctions.**

note making This is a useful skill not only for students, but also for secretaries, journalists and researchers. The best notes are short. If you are making notes on a book, you can usually refer back to the book to fill out a point you are uncertain about. If you are making notes on a lecture, a speech or a discussion it is a mistake to try to get in everything, because all that happens is that you miss the important points and fail to get the general drift of what is being said. Follow the speech closely, noting occasional single words or phrases of importance; keep your eyes on the speaker as much as possible.

Since they are for your eyes only, notes can be in any style you like. People who often need to make notes evolve a shorthand of their own.

Here are some obvious contractions for a start:

Br	British	rt	right
C19	nineteenth century	shd	should
cd	could	t	the
esp	especially	tn	-tion (relatn)
Fr	French	v	very
g	-ing (e.g. reading becomes readg)	wd	would
o	of		
ot	of the		

You can also get into the habit of omitting vowels, and writing the first syllable only of words that are unlikely even in a much shortened form to be mistaken for another word: *org* for *organisation*.

nothing

This is always singular and followed by a singular verb. The possible error is in sentences like

Nothing but meatless dishes *are* available today.

Nothing is the subject of the verb, which should be *is*; but in the example the verb has been attracted into the plural by the nearby *dishes*. This is not a serious mistake. *See* **nobody**.

notices

Road signs must be brief and commanding, like GIVE WAY. But private notices with no force of law and plenty of time for reading are best phrased in a polite way. For example, 'Please keep off — seeds sown' is longer than the rude *Keep Out*, and better also than this one, which was seen in Lincoln's Inn Fields in London:

This ground is temporarily closed for the grass to become re-established after re-instatement.

With notices for sale and similar items of the kind displayed in local post offices it is essential to get in all the necessary facts as briefly as possible, because people simply do not read long notices in which nothing is prominent. The notice below gives all the information needed in the briefest form:

F O R   S A L E

Roller Skates, beginner's size, as new, boxed   £5

12 Abbey Lane

---

nouns

Many nouns can also act as adjectives and verbs:

Garden tools for sale (adj.)

I'll be *gardening* all the afternoon (verb).

When writing it is best generally to choose the short rather than the long word: to say *home* rather than *residence*, and *end* rather than *termination*. *See also* **abstract nouns; agreement; collective nouns; spelling**.

number

This usually takes a plural verb:

A number of passengers *are* waiting for the next plane.
('A number of passengers' [meaning several] is the subject of this sentence and is therefore plural.)

But when it stands for a figure it can have a singular verb:

The number of passes in English *was* reduced by bad spelling.
('The number' [meaning 'the amount'] is the subject of this sentence and is therefore singular.)

numbers

In ordinary writing the tendency is to express figures in words:

He was *seventy-five* years old.

He made a *million* pounds.

His chauffeur was *ten* times happier.

But where precise amounts, dates, sums of money and times are stated, figures are normal:

A ship of 5,000 tons displacement.

There are now 855,000 unemployed.

15th February 1927 was his date of birth.

The rates came to £220 a year.

The bus is due at 14.45.

O

object

In a sentence the name of something on which action is taken is called the *object*:

We painted the *doors*.

They saw *her* in the distance.

Whom have you in mind for the job?

There may be slight difficulty with pronouns. In the sentence:

They will expect you and *me* in good time

the word *me* is correct, because it is the object of *expect*. Learners sometimes use *I*, thinking perhaps that it is right because they would never use it themselves in conversation. In the third example above it is becoming quite common to say *who* instead of *whom*, and it very much looks as if a grammatical error is becoming standard English.

Words that are objects are said to be in the objective case — *him, her, them* for example. Prepositions also cause words to be in the objective case: 'I'll go without *him*'. The objective case is also known as the accusative case. *See* **case; transitive**.

of

A spelling mistake due to recording sound, not sense, and undetected through sheer lack of thought, is *must of* instead of *must have* in sentences like:

I must have left my camera in the coach.

When a noun + of + plural noun is the subject of a verb, the verb is usually singular to go with the singular subject:

A *queue of cars was* waiting at the crossing.

But the tendency is for the verb to be attracted into the plural by the nearby plural noun:

A *flock of geese were* honking at the back door.

This sounds quite acceptable, because one visualises a number of birds each making a noise; whereas in the earlier example the queue of cars is seen and regarded as one thing, like a snake perhaps.

A superfluous *of* sometimes creeps in:

I took it off *of* the table.

officialese   This is the language used by civil servants, local government officials and others for drafting letters, notices and regulations. Such writing has to allow for all sorts of things that might happen, and it has also to anticipate the ingenuity of people who will try to twist a rule to their advantage, or get out of conforming to a regulation. This style cannot help being clumsy and longwinded at times, and it should be kept for occasions when it is really needed.
See **gobbledygook**; **legal language**; **longwindedness**; **padding**; **paraphrase**; **notices**.

on   This can be used to convey the position of something without movement, as in:

The cat's asleep *on* the rug.

It can also indicate movement:

Put your washing *on* top of the pile.

It is best to keep *on* for meanings where no movement is involved, and to use *onto* or *on to* where movement takes place, as in:

He threw the rubbish *onto* the compost heap.

one   This impersonal pronoun is used mainly when the speaker wants to keep himself at a distance and to detach himself from what is being said; for example when he wishes to give advice without poking it directly at his hearer. A parent might say to a child:

Don't put out dirty milk bottles

or he might put it more mildly, in a way less likely to cause resentment:

One just doesn't put out dirty milk bottles.

The possessive form is *one's*:

If one has the misfortune to drop *one's* watch . . .

See **impersonal constructions**.

only Like other adverbs, this must go closely with the word it modifies. In these examples three positions of *only* give three meanings:

Only father paints the frames (nobody else does).

Father *only* paints the frames (he does not make them).

Father paints *only* the frames (he does not paint any other part).

See **adverbs**.

onomatopoeia The term applied to the imitation of sounds by words like *bang, coo, crackle, hum* and *splash.* These lines of Kipling's convey the sound of dockside activity:

And the fenders grind and heave,
And the derricks clack and grate, as the tackle hooks the crate,
And the fall-rope whines through the sheave . . .

opposites The meaning of a word can sometimes be changed to its opposite by adding a prefix, such as *dis-, in-, mis-* and *un-.* For example, *tasteful* becomes *distasteful.* Note also:

*dis*satisfy *in*nocuous *mis*-spell *un*necessary
*dis*sent *in*numerable *mis*shapen *un*natural

When prefixes are attached no letter is dropped, though the *n* of *in-* often melts into the next consonant, to make its easier to say the newly formed word: *ill*egible, *ill*egal, *imm*ortal, *irr*egular.

A less common negative prefix, used mostly in science and medicine, is *a-,* as in *a*pathetic.

Words ending in -ful form their opposites by replacing the *-ful* with *-less; careful* becomes *careless*. Others are *cheerful, harmful, hopeful, merciful, useful*.

order

The meaning of an English sentence depends on the order in which the words are placed: *dog bites man; man bites dog*. In the next example a phrase has been misplaced:

A chesterfield is a piece of furniture made to hold three people with an arm at each end.

And in this one a relative clause has strayed out of place:

We had our lunch sitting on tombstones which consisted of cornish pasties and ginger beer.

Both the mistakes above would have been avoided if the writers had followed the rule that words connected in thought should be kept together.

When a number of events or several descriptive items are found in one sentence, the logical order should be followed. For example, in

The dress material was good, the cutting generously done, the lining well-matched, and the finish perfect.

the various points about the dress start with the material and end with the finish.

The order of words can be used to emphasise a particular idea. In

Homeward the ploughman plods his weary way.

the emphasis falls on *homeward* in its place at the beginning of the sentence. The words could also be arranged: *His weary way the ploughman homeward plods. See* **adverbs**.

-os, -oes   *See* **spelling**.

ought　　　　　This old word now exists only in the present tense:

I *ought* to finish that job first.

If it has to refer to the past, the tense is indicated by putting the infinitive in the past:

I ought *to have finished* that job first.

The negative is *ought not* or *oughtn't*. What it must not have is an auxiliary verb for either tense or negative; *didn't ought* is not permissible.

In meaning it is stronger than *should*:

You ought to visit your grandmother when you're in York.

This suggests that the visit is a duty. But *should* instead of *ought* would make it less obligatory.

over-worked words

Examples are *dramatic*, *luxury*, *marathon*, *overwhelming*, *thunderstruck*. These common examples are from newspapers, where they are used to jack up items of little or no interest into the class of exciting news. They have lost their power through too much use in places where they do not apply. *Marathon* for instance refers originally to the feat of a man who ran 150 miles to seek Spartan aid for Athens against Persian invaders, but it can be applied nowadays to an hour's journey in a powerful vehicle. *See* **clichés**.

overall　　　　This is correctly used of the length of a ship or vehicle, but it is often written pretentiously or for the sake of emphasis where *total*, *general*, *complete* would be better. It often adds nothing and can just be left out, as in:

The *overall* cost of the holiday will be £150.

P

padding   The description applied to words or phrases that
add nothing to a writer's meaning, but are
included to make his message sound more
important than it is. Examples are:

It will be appreciated that . . . (remedy: omit)

It should be noted that . . . (remedy: omit)

Consideration should be given to the possibility
of providing street lighting . . . (remedy: say
'Street lighting should be considered . . .')

Cases in which a shortage of water has
occurred . . . (remedy: say 'Water shortages . . .')

See **dignity words; circumlocution.**

paradox   A statement that apparently contradicts itself,
though true. Statements in this form can drive
the point home:

The worst water shortages of the year occurred
in the great floods of 1952.

paragraph   This is a distinct part of a piece of writing, and
deals with one aspect of the main subject.
Paragraphs nearly always start with a sentence
which tells us what the paragraph is about; the
sentences that follow develop or illustrate the
first one. They should be in some sort of order,
decided by logic or the sequence of events,
so that in a well-knit paragraph it is impossible
to interchange two sentences without spoiling it.
Occasionally this theme or key sentence comes
at the end, to sum up what has been said.
Paragraphs can describe something, or just an
aspect of it; tell part of a story or outline a
complete narrative; develop an argument, or
attack one; or provide an explanation. Here is an
example of a paragraph which starts by stating
what it is about, and then supplies illustrations
as evidence, giving the short examples first:

The potency of television in conditioning youngsters to be loyal enthusiasts of a product, whether they are old enough to consume it or not, became indisputable in the fifties. An ad man taking a marketing class made the casual statement that thanks to TV most children were learning to sing beer and other commercials before they learned to sing the Star-Spangled Banner. Youth Research Institute boasted that even five-year-olds sing beer commercials 'over and over again with gusto.' It pointed out that moppets not only sing the merits of advertised products but do it with the vigour displayed by the most enthusiastic announcers, and do it all day long. They cannot be turned off as a set can. When TV was in its infancy, an ad alerted manufacturers to the extraordinary ability of TV to etch messages on young brains: 'Where else on earth is brand consciousness fixed so firmly in the minds of four-year-old tots? What is it worth to a manufacturer who can close in on this juvenile audience and continue to sell to it year after year, right up to its attainment of adulthood and fully-fledged buyer status?'

adapted from: Vance Packard,
The Hidden Persuaders

Newspapers and novels often paragraph less rigidly to provide shorter units that are easy to take in. The example above, if reproduced in a newspaper, might be split up into about three very short paragraphs.

paraphrase   A simpler version of a passage of prose or verse, written to explain the meaning of the original to someone who might find it difficult. The writing of a paraphrase makes the writer of it really think about the passage he is working on; it is a good way to get at the heart of the meaning. Outside the study or the classroom paraphrase is used every day, for example in newspapers. Imagine that a government report is published on chemicals in food, for preserving, colouring and flavouring the 'fresh' foods we buy, telling us why they are put in, whether it is for our benefit or the profit of the processing firm, whether they are dangerous or not, and whether they impair the nourishment value of the food. It will be written in scientific language, with the aid of many statistics; so the journalist's job is choose the main points and put them in shortened form in ordinary language for the benefit of the general reader. Again (as we mentioned in the entry on *legal language*) government regulations have to be drawn up in such a way that there is no possible doubt about the meaning and no loophole left for anyone to evade it. The new regulation will also have to mention all the older ones it is replacing; one cannot have two sets of rules on the same subject. All this means writing at length in official language, so in such cases the government department concerned will provide a simplified version for the guidance of the ordinary citizen.

The first verse of Blake's 'The Tyger' is followed by a suggested paraphrase:

Tyger! Tyger! burning bright
In the forests of the night,
What immortal hand or eye
Could frame thy fearful symmetry?

Tiger, your brilliance resembles a fire gleaming in the forest-like darkness of the night. What god could have designed and shaped your symmetrical form, which inspires fear in those who see it?

The first point one notices is that a splendid piece of writing, powerful in sound and rhythmic movement, has been destroyed — or so it looks. But a paraphrase is not intended to be as good as, or in any way the equivalent of the original. It is an interpretation of part of the meaning, and once made it can be scrapped. Here the person making the paraphrase has been made to think. A tiger does not really burn, but with its power and colour it has something of the force and brightness and warmth of a fire at night; and this has to be brought out by turning the metaphor *burning* into a simile: 'Your brilliance *resembles* (Or *is like*) a fire'. Then does 'forests of the night' mean a real but very dark forest, or a night which has the darkness of deep, sunless forest? Note also that sentences are broken up into shorter units, so that points can be understood one at a time; and that the paraphrase is longer than the original, as one would expect.

If you are required to make a paraphrase, use language as simple as possible. Simplify long sentences by breaking them up into shorter sentences. Turn metaphors into similes; e.g. *Misfortune dogged us* will become *Ill-luck followed us as closely as a hound follows a scent*. Omit nothing; explain or simplify everything. Do not be afraid of writing at greater length than that of the original.

parenthesis   An aside inserted into a main sentence:

They told me (and I could well believe it) that there'd been no rain for two years.

We crossed in the new boat – the old one having developed engine trouble – with a very large party of pilgrims.

The Manchester group, consisting of Dan and Charles and Damian, is at present rehearsing.

As in the examples above, parentheses can be marked off by pairs of brackets, dashes or commas. If a parenthesis is opened with a bracket it must be closed with a bracket, and so on; and it must be closed, or it will get mixed up with the main sentence. A parenthesis can be taken out of a sentence without damaging its structure and meaning, as in the examples above.

Too long a parenthesis, or too many of them, hold up the drift of what the writer has to say, and this can be trying to the reader.
See **brackets; commas, 3**.

participles There are two kinds in English. The *past* participle ends in *d* or *t*, as in *shaped, found, dealt, taught*; or in *n*, as in *broken, given, seen, torn*.

The *present* participle ends in *-ing*; *sleeping, writing*. (Note that when *-ing* is added to a word ending in silent *e*, the *e* usually drops out, as in *ride, riding*; and that when *-ing* is added to a stressed vowel and consonant, the consonant doubles to take the weight of the stress, as in: *tap, tapping; fit, fitting; prefer, preferring*.)

There are two uses of the present participle that grammarians tend to disapprove of.

1 In the sentence:

Coming home late, we found the house very cold.

the participle *coming* is attached to *we*, and that is correct. But in

Sitting drowsily in the sun sipping our coffee, a large black cat rubbed against our legs.

the participle *sitting* has nothing to attach itself to, except the cat which was unlikely to be sipping 'our' coffee. The meaning of the writer is clear, but the grammar is shaky, and strictly speaking the sentence should be altered to: *As we were sipping* . . . This grammatically incorrect usage is described as the floating participle; a few years ago it would have been considered a mistake, but it is less and less likely to be reckoned a serious error.

2 In this sentence, spoken by a parent:

I don't like you coming home so late at nights.

what the speaker dislikes is the *coming home late*, but from the grammar point of view *you* is the object of *like*, making it seem as if the speaker dislikes the person he is speaking to — which is clearly untrue. In order to put the sentence right from their point of view, the grammarians would like it to be altered thus:

I don't like your coming home so late at nights.

Here the object of *like* is *coming*, and there is no possible doubt. However the 'mistake' we have just looked at, like the previous one, is much made by distinguished writers, and is most unlikely to cause much trouble today.

parts of speech

It is worth recalling that in English many words can act as two or three parts of speech:

Please *paint* the front door. (verb)
I'll pay for the *paint* (noun)
and the *paint*-brushes. (adj.)

See **adjective, adverb, conjunction, exclamation mark, noun, pronoun and verb.**

passed, past

Keep *passed* for the verb:

Hours *passed* without a breath of wind.
She *passed* her test.

Use *past* for all other purposes:

Half-*past* five.
Pop stars are *past* it at twenty-two.

For sale – *past* exam papers.

Just a few yards *past* the post office.

passive   *See* **active and passive**.

percentage   This is best kept for use where a proportion of
                  a hundred is intended:

                  77 is a much lower *percentage* of successes
                  than last year.

                  It is liable to be used loosely for dignity
                  purposes:

                  A very high percentage of motorists will not
                  re-license this year.

                  In the last example *most* would do as well or
                  better than the words italicised.

periphrasis   A roundabout way of saying things. *See*
                  longwindedness; officialese.

person   The grammatical term used in describing
                  pronouns, and for some parts of verbs:

First person	*Second person*	*Third person*
I am	You are	He is
We are	You are	They are
Me	You	Them

                  As a noun *person* tends to be rather formal
                  and official: 'All persons must be in possession
                  of a valid ticket'. *People* is the word for
                  ordinary conversation.

phrase   A group of words that can act as a noun,
                  adjective or verb:

                  Travelling light with little luggage is advisable.
                  (noun)

                  Members *with green tickets* come this way.
                  (adjective)

With a deep sigh the dog subsided on the mat. (adverb)

By themselves phrases do not make complete sense; they cannot be separated by full-stops, like sentences. In this piece of teenage writing, note the phrase wrongly standing by itself, as if it were a sentence, but without a main verb:

To stay alive we must find a new planet, somewhere we can begin a new life. *Going outside our own galaxy at the speed of light.*

To improve it the words *going outside* must be replaced by *we shall go outside*. It is a very common error to use phrases by themselves without a main verb, and good writers do this on purpose. But candidates for examinations should make sure that anything standing between full-stops has a main verb. *See* **sentences**.

plural words   The words below stand for things made up of two parts. The words are plural in form, and take a plural verb, but if used with *a pair of*, the verb is singular:

There *is a pair* of trousers in the top drawer.

pincers   pliers   shears   tweezers   scissors
goggles   glasses   spectacles   boots   braces
briefs   garters   gloves   knickers   pants
shoes   shorts   slippers   socks   suspenders
tights   trousers

plurals   Some special cases are:
Words ending in -*um*. These come from Latin, and a few of them have kept their Latin plural: *Addendum, addenda*; *datum, data*. The general tendency is to make them plural by adding *s*; *aquariums, premiums*. Some seem to be halfway: you can say *memorandums* or *memoranda*, depending on which sounds best to you.

Words ending in -*on*. *Automaton, criterion* and *phenomenon* officially form their plural in -*a*, like *criteria*, but increasingly they are treated like normal English words, and have their plural in *s*.

Words ending in -*us*. Most of them form their plural with -*es*, like *bonuses, buses, prospectuses*. But a few keep their Latin plural, as in *radii, stimuli, tumuli*.

Words ending in -*is*. *Analysis, basis, oasis* and a few others change the -*is* to -*es*: *crisis, crises*.

Finally, a miscellaneous group of plurals to remember: *handfuls, handkerchiefs, lay-bys, spoonfuls, trade unions*. *See* **spelling 3**; *also end of entry on* **idioms**.

poetry

The most effective form of expression and communication. Concentrated, subtle and flexible, it can get more meaning, and more kinds of meaning, into a few words than any other medium. It does this by means of metre, rhythm, sound and imagery. *See* **figurative language**; **metaphor**; **rhythm**.

possessive case

A noun in the possessive case tells us that the person or thing referred to owns or is connected with something:

Eileen's cycle needs a new chain.
This *month's* figures show a great improvement.
East Africa is a *naturalist's* paradise.

Possession is shown by '*s* or *s*'; *see* **apostrophe, 2.**

postcards

These should have the date and the writer's address, but no opening or closing words — no 'Dear Sir' or 'Yours faithfully'. They are informal and should not be used for anything private or formal, such as correspondence with a business, or prospective employer.

practice, practise

Practice is the noun; *practise* is the verb. Remember the difference by *advice* (noun), *advise* (verb). American English uses only *practice*.

practice, value of

Any skill is improved by the right kind of practice. So far as English is concerned, the nearer practice comes to real life, the better. Keeping a diary, acting as secretary to a club or committee, writing letters are examples. Without writing unnecessarily, look for opportunities to practise letters: e.g. to makers of goods about their quality, price, workmanship, design; to local councillors, M.P.s, officials of organisations; to the B.B.C., magazines, the Press. In England we have one of the highest postal rates in the world, and this is partly because people just put up with it without complaining. We also have some of the world's worst newspapers, as well as the best, and this again is partly due to the fact that proprietors and editors are in touch only with a section of their readers. In these and other cases consumers could improve things by making their views and wishes and ideas clearly and forcefully known.

précis

A condensed version of a passage of prose, intended to make clear the essential contents of the original to a person who has not read it. The making of a précis was formerly a part of most examinations in English language, though in recent years the term has gone out of use, and candidates are required to produce summaries. The difference is that a précis is a scaled-down version of a passage, while a summary may concentrate on selecting specified material, such as evidence or arguments in favour of a particular point: *see* **summary**.

Competence in précis-writing is largely a matter of practice. The method suggested is:

1 Read the passage quickly to get a general idea of what it is about.

2 Give it one or more slower readings; and when you are getting hold of it underline the important points and connecting links. Look over these marked points, find the backbone of the passage and see how everything fits on to it.

3 Make a rough draft without looking at the original, except the underlined points. The memory is a very good sieve of what is important, and the less you look at the original the more completely you will be able to recast it in your own words.
The rough draft stage may have to be omitted; practice for the examination will decide whether you are likely to have time for this.

4 Read the rough draft and write the final version, when you have made sure: **a** that it is clear and connected and reads well;   **b** that nothing important has been left out; and **c** that it is not too long.

The examiners will wish to see the main points or chief facts or the line of thought brought out; the sequence of ideas must be shown by the way in which your own sentences are connected. Examples of connecting methods are:

These proposals (or aims, or actions, or events) . . .	In fact . . .
	Actually . . .
	However . . .
To achieve this . . .	

The result of . . . was	But nowadays . . .
The next step . . .	Moreover . . .
Eventually . . .	In addition. . .
In the end . . .	Another reason . . .
Therefore . . .	

What the candidate must not do is just to pick out the important sentences and write them down without links; a version on these lines shows that the reader has not grappled with and understood the passage. To make sure that the candidate understands the writing before him, the instructions commonly advise him to use his own words. Nothing reveals a candidate's failure to understand a passage so much as a number of sentences or groups of words taken over from the original without alteration.

Below is an example, a fairly difficult one, of a passage for précis. It contains just over 300 words, which you should try to reduce to about 100 words, using the method suggested above. Then read the précis provided, and the comments. It does not matter if your version is different; it may well be better.

Holidays, medieval and modern

One curious result of the Industrial Revolution can claim a special place in this chronicle of the relationship between men and their land. For the medieval peasant eight weeks of the year were holy days, days when a service in the parish church was followed by freedom for rest and celebration. Each chosen black- and red-letter day, each Church festival, was a part of the wheel of the year and served for rites so much more ancient than Christianity as to be almost as old as the consciousness of man. No countryman could have celebrated them away from his own cottage, fields and animals, his

neighbours and his church, for they were
important threads in the fabric of life where all
these things were woven together in a single
design.

Now the sharp division of work from play and
the natural from the supernatural has turned
holy days into holidays, and the compelling
restlessness and ugliness of towns has made
holidays an occasion for escape from home.
So there is this new form of mass migration —
no longer for fishing or fowling or the visiting
of shrines. Instead a flight from a man-made
world too hard, dirty and hideous to allow its
inhabitants to rest, to lie down on the ground or
to dance upon it, to turn back to their
surroundings for refreshment. Three hundred
years ago how impossible it would have seemed
that England should be cumbered with towns
built as an escape from towns, that half its
south and east coasts should be encrusted with
red bricks, walled behind concrete, the sea
itself grasped after with iron piers. If the
migrations have largely defeated their purpose by
spreading more hardness and a new ugliness,
at least the resorts are clean, and human beings
can find just room enough to stretch their bodies
on the sand.

                         Jacquetta Hawkes, *A Land*

**Please do not read the version below till you
have made your own shortening of the passage
above.**

The Industrial Revolution made a distinct change
in the relationship between man and his
environment. The medieval peasant enjoyed fifty
six holy days a year, when after a church service,
no work was done. These holy days were an
integral part of life and were essentially local.

But now, as a result of changes in work and

religion, holy days have become holidays. The environment has become so unsuitable for rest and recreation that people want to get away from their homes. Consequently the coast is ringed with towns built as escapes from other towns; they may be ugly, but they do provide access to the sea.

Comments

1 The reduced version is on the long side at 106 words. Is any further shortening possible?

2 Should there be some connecting link after the opening sentence, such as 'notably in the matter of holidays'?

3 What is summed up by   **a** 'an integral part of life' and   **b** 'essentially local'?

4 Note the contrast and connection provided by 'But now . . .'

5 Note what is summed up by 'unsuitable for rest and recreation'.

6 Note how 'consequently' links 'want to get away' with 'as escapes'.

prefer   This word is followed by *to*:

She prefers *jam* to honey.

A common mistake, and one to be avoided, is to say *She prefers jam than honey*. If the infinitive of a verb is introduced, we have to say *rather than*:

Really I'd prefer to do some canoeing rather than go for a walk.

prefixes   These are small groups of letters, mostly from Latin or Greek, placed in front of words to alter their meaning, as in: *co-operate*, *disconnect*. Anyone using or learning English eventually knows what all the following prefixes mean; it is best to learn them as one comes across them, rather than to memorise the list.

prefix	*meaning*	*examples*
a, ab, abs	away, from	avert, abnormal, abstract
ad	to	admit, adhere, attach
ante	before	antecedent, antediluvian, ante-room
auto	self	automatic, autograph
bene	good	benefactor, beneficial
bi	twice, two	bicycle, biplane, biennial, biscuit
circum	round	circumference, circumspect
co, com, con	together	co-education, communicate, concentric
contra	against	contradict, contrary
de	down, from	depress, descent
dis	not, apart	disappear, disinter, different
ex, e	out of	eccentric, extract, eliminate
fore	before	forecast, foreman, foresee
hyper	over, in excess	hyper-inflation, hyper-market, hypercritical
in	in, into	include, ingress, import
in	not	inefficient, illegal, impossible, irrational
inter	between	international, interrupt
male	bad	malevolent, malnutrition
micro	small	microphone, microscope
mis	wrong	misfire, misfit, misuse
ob	against	obstacle, obstruct
peri	round	periphery, periscope
poly	many	polyglot, polytechnic
post	after	postpone, postmortem
pre	before	predict, prepare, preface
pro	forward	promote, progress

re	again, back	repeat, return, re-wind
sub	under	substandard, submarine
syn	together	synthetic, synchronise, sympathy
tele	distant	teleprinter, telephone, television
trans	across	transcontinental, transmit
un	not	unfit, unhappy, unsafe
vice	instead of	vice-consul, vice-president

prepositions   These cause pronouns to be in the objective (or accusative) case:

Are you coming *with me*?

Keep seats *for us*.

He beckoned *to her*.

Note that if a preposition governs two pronouns, or a noun and a pronoun, both must be in the objective case:

It was clear *to him* and *me*.

They sent a taxi for *Angela* and *us*.

It is in order to end a sentence with a preposition:

Who are you going *with*?

What's this gadget *for*?

A number of nouns and verbs are followed by particular prepositions. The list below includes some of the common usages:

agree to (a plan)	disgusted at (a thing)
agree with (a person)	disgusted with (a person)
aim at	equal to
angry with (a person)	full of
ashamed of	guilty of

averse from

blame for

comment on

compared with, to

complain of

congratulate on

contrast with
(contrast as a noun,
with accent on the first
syllable, can be followed
by *between or with*)

die of

differ from

identical with

independent of

inspired by

liable to

oblivious of

opposite to

regard for

rely on

similar to

suffer from

sympathise with

tendency to

worthy of

**Note also, that prepositions are often more
efficient and more economical than phrases.
For example, in:**

More progress has been made *in the case of*
Manchester *with regard to* housing than *in the
case of* any other city.

**the prepositions *by*, *in* and *by* (in that order)
would be much better than the italicised
phrases. The phrases below should normally be
replaced by the bracketed prepositions:**

in respect of (of)
in relation to (towards, with)
with regard to (in, to)

**Certain prepositions are attached to verbs to
give them distintive meanings, e.g. *about,
away, by, down, in, off, on, out, over, through,
up*. Here are some examples of such linkages:**

dig down   dig in   dig over   dig up

go away   go down   go in   go off   go on
go out   go over   go through   go up

hand down   hand in   hand off   hand on
hand over   hand round

When there is no object the addition should go next to its verb:

Get *out* before the roof caves *in*!

Hurry *up* if you want to get *away* by five.

When there is an object, the addition comes after it:

Get your bikes *out*.

Hurry them *up*.

Though when the object is a noun — not a pronoun — the preposition can go in front of the object:

Get *out* your bikes.

Blow *up* the tyres.

With long and awkward objects the verb and its addition should be kept together; the objects are bracketed in these examples:

Please put *away* (anything in the nature of rubbish).

We'll send *down* (all the things we shan't need on the voyage).

presentation of work

Number questions, with titles if necessary; do not overdo underlining; give what is needed, no more.

Write up to the margin.

Do not use ampersands or *etc*.

Be sparing with colloquialism.

See **writing**.

principal, principle

Princi*pal* is a person (remember it by the ending); *principle* is a basic rule.

pro forma

This is a piece of pomposity used by officials and others when they mean simply a *form*.

pronouns

As their name implies, these words stand for nouns and thereby save a great deal of tedious repetition in writing. There are three main kinds:

1 *Personal*

		1st person	*2nd person*	*3rd person*
Singular	Nominative	I	You	he she it
	Objective	me	you	him her it
	Genitive	mine	yours	his hers its
Plural	Nominative	we	you	they
	Objective	us	you	them
	Genitive	ours	yours	theirs

In this group we include the reflexive pronouns, so-called because they refer back to the subject of the sentence:

I can see *myself* in a year's time . . .
They found *themselves* in a difficulty.

The singular ones are: *myself, yourself, himself*; and the plural ones: *ourselves, yourselves, themselves.*

Reflexive pronouns are also used for emphasis:

I repaired the engine *myself.*

See **-self**.

2 *Demonstrative*

These point out something or someone. The

singular ones are *this* and *that*; the plural, *these* and *those*.

3 *Relative and interrogative*

These are used for connecting, or for asking questions:

Would people *who* keep brief-cases in lockers please collect them.

Which model do you prefer?

		For people	*For things*
Singular	Nominative	who	which, what
and plural	Objective	whom	which, what
	Genitive	whose	which

That is also used as a relative pronoun:

The car *that* I saw had a shattered windscreen.

Put the noun first, then the pronoun, so that there is no doubt:

When *Jane* went to the post-office, *she* found it closed.

(Not: 'When she went . . ., Jane found it closed')

Be careful to avoid ambiguity:

The starter gripped his pistol, bent his head down, and let it off.

pronunciation The letter *c* can be pronounced in three ways. Hard: s*c*eptic, e*cc*entric, va*cc*inate; soft: abs*c*ess, iras*c*ible, e*cc*entric, va*cc*inate; and like *ch* in *cello*.
ch can be hard, like *k*: *Chaos*, *chiropodist*, *hierarchy*, *loch*; or soft, like *sh*: *brochure*, *chagrin*, *charlatan*, *nonchalant*.
And a few importations with their pronunciation in brackets: *bona fide* (bona fydy), *coup* (coo), *debris* (daybree), *maestro* (mystro). *See* **accent**; **spelling**.

Proof correcting

Anyone may be called on to correct the rough copy which the printer of a programme, fixture card, catalogue or booklet supplies to the person who has ordered it. If you have to send such material to a printer, make sure that it is accurate and legible; alterations can be very expensive. For correcting proofs, use the symbols that printers understand; they can be found in many reference books, such as *Pears' Cyclopaedia,* or in a leaflet supplied by the British Federation of Master Printers, 11, Bedford Row, London, W.C.1. *See* **italics.**

proportion

This word should be kept for expressing the relationship of parts to wholes:

In 1976 a *larger proportion* of candidates passed than in 1975.

It should not be used to mean *many* or *most*:

A *large proportion of* (most) customers use cheques.

protagonist

The chief actor in a drama of any kind; even in a battle you cannot have two protagonists.

proverbs

These are comments and ideas, made in the conversation of ordinary people, that have become accepted as wise and sensible, and so passed into the language for use on suitable occasions. Sometimes they conveniently express an idea better than the speaker can, and help him to produce a wise-sounding thought: 'There's no smoke without fire'. Very commonly they are consoling, and help the speaker to put up with a misfortune: 'It's a long lane that has no turning'. They can appear to contradict each other:

Too many cooks spoil the broth.
Many hands make light work.

punctuation

The oldest known writing is found in the form of carved inscriptions, incised clay tablets and ancient battered manuscripts. They have one feature in common; lack of punctuation. The writing runs straight on, and it must have been difficult to understand. Eventually a number of marks were devised to assist writing to attain the clearness of the spoken word. Two of them merely indicate the tone of voice of the speaker: the *question mark* and the *exclamation mark*; they help the written word to reproduce the sound of a question, or of surprise or alarm. Quotation marks can also indicate the way in which words should be read.

The remaining punctuation marks are discussed in their own entries: *full-stop, comma, colon, semi-colon, dash, hyphen, quotation marks, apostrophe, brackets*. These are meant to enable a writer to make his meaning clear, and they should supply this aid unobtrusively, smoothing the reader's path without his being aware of it.

Full-stops should be used fairly generously; they are basic, dividing up written matter into units that are easy to take in. It is a good idea to re-read work, as if aloud; and this will show, not only where full-stops are needed, but also where they can be omitted or replaced. Short sentences are readable, but too many short sentences can be very trying to the reader. The commonest error with full-stops is to omit them where needed.

Next in importance is the *comma*, which serves a variety of purposes. We repeat the advice that it must not be used to separate complete sentences: 'He buys ballpoints by the dozen, he uses nothing else'. In expressions like this the comma must be supplemented by a conjunction (e.g. *because*), or replaced by a *semi-colon*. The latter stop is useful for separating two sentences (like those in the example just given) which are about the same subject, and so do not need the decisive break indicated by a full-stop.

Competence in punctuating comes from familiarity with a number of sentence-patterns; and this familiarity is acquired through reading and listening.

Q

question mark   This (?) is placed at the end of a direct question:

Have you heard the news?

It acts like a full-stop; a capital letter is needed for the next sentence.

Polite requests are sometimes put in the form of a question:

Will you let us know your arrival time?

and then they are usually, but not always, followed by a question mark. In such requests there is probably a tendency for a full-stop to be used instead of a question mark.

Question marks are sometimes used in brackets to express the writer's doubts or wish to be funny:

He bought an old car (?) which he is now repairing.

This usage is best avoided.

question, whether

The correct usage is:

The question whether she qualifies will soon be settled.

Not 'the question *of* whether . . .', or 'the question *as to* whether'.

questions

There are two main kinds: *direct*, and *indirect*. Direct questions reproduce word for word what has been asked:

Where on earth are my gloves?

They are formed by putting the subject after the verb instead of before it; and as stated above they need a question mark.

Indirect, or *reported,* questions are in this form:

The customs officer asked me what I had paid for the watch.

Note that no question mark is required; it is a mistake to insert one.

In addition there are direct questions that expect no answer; they are used for example to make an argument or statement sound more convincing:

Whoever would have thought it?

And what, may I ask, are the Opposition doing about it?

They are known as rhetorical questions, because they are commonly used by public speakers.

quicker

This word is primarily the comparative form of the adjective *quick*, but it is also used as an adverb:

In heavy traffic you can get there quicker on foot.

See **adverbs**.

quotation marks

These are a comparatively late addition to the list of devices for punctuation, and they are well-established; though one authority (G. H. Vallins) writes: 'one of the simplest and most beneficial reforms in English would be their total abolition'. His dislike was probably due to the fact that it is

difficult to draw up tidy rules for using them.
The basic rule is that the quotation marks enclose
what was actually spoken:

'To-day's coach is booked up', said the clerk.

Note, as well as the quotation marks, the comma
after *up*. When a piece of direct speech is
broken up by such words as 'he added', 'she
replied' and so on, the inserted words are
comma-ed off, as if they were in brackets:

'There's no point', she went on, 'in catching the
early train.'

When the inserted words are put in at a point
where there is a stop in the original, that stop is
retained. For example:

'The small hall will do; we haven't sold enough
tickets for the big one.'

becomes:

'The small hall will do', he said; 'we haven't
sold enough tickets for the big one.'

The semi-colon that followed *do* in the original
is placed after *he said* in the quoted form.

Single quotation marks(' . . . ') are the most
commonly used nowadays; double quotation
marks are kept for quotations within quotations,
thus:

'We expect a big "yes" in the referendum', he
added.

Note that where passages of dialogue occur in a
story, every speech starts with a fresh paragraph:

'Ransome', I asked abruptly, 'how long have I
been on deck? I am losing the notion of
time.'

'Fourteen days, sir', he said. 'It was a fortnight
last Monday since we left the anchorage.'

Then I noticed the broad shadow on the horizon.

See **dialogue**.

quotations   When a piece of verse, or more than a sentence or two of prose, is to be quoted, it is best to let the passage stand out by writing it as a separate paragraph.

R

raise, rise   *Raise* is transitive and must have an object:

The firemen *raised the escape* to the fifth floor.

Rise is intransitive:

Wages *rose* even faster than prices.

Note the correct form of the noun:

An increase in pay is called a *rise*.

re   This word is half a Latin phrase, *in re*. It belongs to legal language and is best left there. It is not a good alternative to *about*.

reason, it stands to

In an argument this is often a sign that the speaker is being unreasonable.

reason was   The correct usage is:

He was late. The reason was *that* his bicycle chain broke.

The common mistake is to say 'The reason was because . . .'. From the grammar point of view *reason* is a noun, and is followed by the relative pronoun *that*. *Because* is a conjunction, and is correctly used to link a sentence and a clause.

He was late, because his bicycle chain broke.

See **because**.

recipient   Do not say 'He was the recipient of a silver cup',
                       instead of *he received* . . . or *he was given* . . .
                       See **active and passive**.

redundant words
                       In the sentence 'I met *up with* some friends' the
                       words in italics are not needed; they add no
                       meaning to *met*. A similar redundancy is found
                       in expressions such as 'co-operate together',
                       where *together* merely repeats what has already
                       been said in the *co-* of co-operate. Other
                       examples are:

                       I can't seem to be able to . . . (I seem unable
                       too . . .)

                       check *up on*

                       face *up to*

                       forecast of our *future* needs

                       mix *together*

                       recur *again*

                       The words in italics merely repeat what has
                       already been said. *See* **tautology**.

reference   Those who have to fill application forms for
                       employment should note that this word does
                       not mean *testimonial*; it means the reply sent to
                       a potential employer by a person who has
                       agreed to act as a referee for a candidate.

reflexive pronouns
                       See **pronouns**.

regard to, with, as regards
                       About or *concerning* should be used instead
                       of these weak phrases.

relative pronouns
                       See **pronouns**.

relatively   The word should be used only in expressions where the idea of comparison is present, as it is in this example:

She is *relatively* young for such responsibility.

She is being compared with other holders of responsible posts. *See* **comparatively**.

repetition

The reiteration of a word or phrase for emphasis can be very effective, as in the opening chapter of *Bleak House,* where the repeated *fog* brings home the choking effect that Dickens wanted. In ordinary writing too much accidental repetition can make the work look somewhat threadbare, and here the writer can find help in the great variety of synonyms that is offered by English. For example, instead of saying 'The *match* was twenty minutes old when . . .' a reporter could use such words as *play, game, contest, tie, battle, fixture*, according to the context. The use of synonyms to avoid duplication of a nearby word always brings about an improvement.

For example:

We took the upper *road*, but progress on this *road* was slow because the *road* was covered with loose chippings.

This reads better if the repetition of *road* is avoided, thus;

We took the upper *road*, but progress on *it* was slow because the *surface* was covered with loose chippings.

See **variety**.

reported speech

See **direct speech** ; **questions**.

respectively

This is correctly used to link closely two series of items:

Janet, Betty and Eileen are going to Spain, Scotland and Norway *respectively*.

The word sorts them out to their holiday destinations. It is however often added to a sentence to make it sound dignified:

We shall vote for our respective candidates.

All the writer means here is 'We shall vote for our own candidates'.

right   The normal form of the adverb from *right* is *rightly*:

Ann was *rightly* chosen as our representative.

But when the adverb follows the verb, *right* is the normal usage:

The puzzle won't come out *right*.

S

same   The word occurs in business letters instead of the pronouns *it* or *this*:

We acknowledge receipt of your order for a Said Eight settee. *Same* will be delivered in about eight weeks' time.

This usage sounds clumsy and old-fashioned, and it is better to stick to the simple *it* or *this*.

sarcasm   There may be a place for this, though it is too commonly used by people in authority to show their superiority:

That wasn't very clever of you, was it?

It can easily make the user sound sour and unpleasant, and is therefore best avoided.

save   This word has been wrecked by mis-use. It means to conserve resources by storing them in a bank etc., but commonly it is used to mean *spend money at once on*. If you respond to the invitation 'Save £5 on this special offer suit at £35' you are saving nothing at all; you are £35 poorer.

scarcely   This is a near-negative word, correctly used in:

I have scarcely any cash.

It is incorrect to add a further negative:

I have scarcely *no* cash.
I have*n't* scarcely any cash.

See **hardly.**

Scotch, Scots, Scottish
It is best to keep *Scotch* for things, and use *Scots* and *Scottish* for people.

selecting material
See **material.**

-self   The correct forms of the -self pronouns are:

myself   ourselves   yourself   yourselves
himself, herself   itself   themselves.

In addition there is *oneself*. Note that *hisself* and *theirselves* are mistakes; and that it is poor English to say:

Buy tickets for your sister and *self.*

Yourself is required here. *See* **pronouns, 1**

semi-colons   This stop is placed between two sentences that are about the same subject, but are grammatically complete and can stand on their own:

He took the book back to the shop; there were sixteen pages missing.

The old hospital should be closed as soon as possible; it is very difficult to keep it clean.

The semi-colon can also be used to slow down a sequence of sentences, phrases or words, so

that the reader considers each item a little longer
than would be possible if commas were used:

I shall take with me a rucksack; a sleeping bag;
cooking equipment; a geological hammer; and
some emergency rations.

sentences

These are complete units of expression, standing
on their own, and conveying a clear meaning to
the reader or listener. The verb is the essential
part of a sentence, and a sentence cannot exist
without one. For example:

At the end of the day, a sleepy ride home in a
warm crowded bus

is not a sentence because there is no verb, and
thus no subject; we do not know who the
sentence refers to or what happened. However
if we add *we quite enjoyed* after *day* the
sentence is complete and there is no doubt about
the action, who is concerned, and when. The
verbless example we gave above is a phrase, and
it is quite a common fault for writers to employ
phrases as if they were complete sentences:

There was a lot to do on our first day at the
Tech. in Collier Road. Such as registering and
getting timetables and a plan of the building.

The words from *Such* to the end have no main
verb and do not constitute a sentence. The
solution is either to make it a sentence by
saying 'We had to register and get timetables . . .'
or to replace the full-stop after *Collier Road* by
a dash. If the latter is adopted, *such* will need a
small *s*. *See* **clauses; order; phrases; main
verb**.

shades of meaning

With its enormous vocabulary English is able to
record fine shades of meaning. In a trade or
craft many people make these fine distinctions
every day of their lives, when they select a

special tool with a special name for a particular job; and seedsman's catalogues may describe hundreds of different roses. People with extensive vocabularies at their disposal acquire them gradually, by practice, not by learning off lists; and by practice we all come to know the difference between the words in such pairs as:

reside, live   social, sociable   surprised, amazed
restive, restless   skilled, skilful   fellow-feeling,
sympathy

See **synonyms**.

shall, will

The future tense in English is expressed by auxiliary verbs, thus:

I *shall* go   you *will* go   he/she *will* go
we *shall* go   you *will* go   they *will* go

Note that if *will* is used with the first person (*I, we*) it conveys *wish* and *determination*:

I *will* get that job done, however long its takes.

similar, like

Like is the commoner word, and is useful since it can be used both as an adjective:

My camera's *like* yours,

and as an adverb:

A centrifuge works *like* a milk churn.

similar is sometimes used as a dignity word; it is most at home in text-books, especially of science, where it has an air of exactness that is appropriate.

similes

These are comparisons in which a person or thing or action is likened to something else to make the speaker's meaning clear. In Dickens' *Great Expectations* a man and a boy are given a hurried breakfast because the housewife wants to get on with preparing Christmas dinner:

We had our slices served out, *as if* we were two thousand troops on a forced march.

The simile starts with the words *as if*, and it brings out the haste, the compulsory nature and the parade-ground aspect of the operation.

Similes usually start with such expressions as: *like, as, as if, as though, faster than*. There are hundreds of them invented every day; some just serve the needs of the speaker and then are forgotten, while others pass into the language. And then the latter keep their freshness for a time, but end up by being tired and battered, so that they cannot do much work and perhaps go into retirement. Examples of the overworked simile are: *as cool as a cucumber*; *like water off a duck's back*; *as poor as a church mouse*; *as sound as a bell*; and scores of others. *See* **figurative language**.

simple as that   The expression 'It's as simple as that' is rarely quite true.

simplicity   In general, this should be the aim of writing (complicated material, however, may need a difficult set of words, and fine shades of meaning may necessitate longer, less common words). Most of us suffer from the temptation to use too many and too long words. 'Be worried', if you like, but do not 'view with grave disquiet'; have 'talks', but do not get 'involved in deliberations'; and if you want to get away for a holiday, by all means 'escape', but do not delay to 'make good your escape'.

singular or plural
Most of the difficulties are dealt with under *collective nouns, nothing, number, of, plural, spelling, there*. Therefore under this heading only a reminder that the real subject decides whether the verb is singular or plural. In:

About one in ten children *goes* to a university

goes is correct because the subject is the singular *one*. The common and understandable error is to write *go*, the verb being attracted into the plural by the neighbouring plural word *children*. Again in:

One of those people who *believe* the newspapers

believe is correctly plural because the subject *who* is plural. The very natural mistake is to write *believes*, but it is not a mistake that will be penalised in an examination, even if it is noticed.

slang

The word is applied to new and lively expressions introduced into conversation, mainly by young people. It can add life and variety and amusement to language, but it should not normally be used in writing, except in letters to friends. One reason is that slang may seem undignified in some kinds of prose; for example it would not be suitable in making an application for a passport or driving licence. More important is the fact that slang starts by being the private language of a locality or group of people — students, engineers, scientists, for example — and therefore will read like a foreign language, as in this example:

The lid was off. He'd done a screwy thing. Whether he tried the chopper or the tin bird he'd join the crazy junkie in the car and he wouldn't be springing for a long time.

Some of the best slang becomes permanent and joins the ranks of standard English. The following, for instance, were once slang but seem now quite acceptable:

to jump at a job

a dead-end occupation

going full-blast

getting bogged-down

See **colloquialisms**.

slogans   These are short phrases or sentences used in
                     advertising and politics, designed to stick in
                     the reader's mind by constant reiteration. They
                     are rarely completely true; anything so brief is
                     bound to be liable to exceptions.
                     'Drinkapintamilka' may be recommending a
                     product that is not good for some people; and
                     it is easy to think of other examples that are
                     only half-true. No intelligent person is taken in
                     by any slogan, though he may be amused by
                     one.

small, little   Normally *small* describes size, and *little*
                     describes quantity.

snarl words   *See* **feeling in words**. A number of words
                     convey the speaker's dislike of what he is
                     talking about, rather than any factual meaning.
                     Examples from various parts of the world are:
                     bourgeois, *egg-head*, *nigger*, *trippers*, *yid*.
                     They can be dangerous in muddying a
                     discussion, arousing prejudice, and feeding
                     mind-less hatreds.

sort of   It is better to use *rather* in such expressions as:

                     I felt *sort of* sleepy.

                     The phrase suggests that the user is not quite
                     clear about his meaning; it gives the impression
                     of vagueness.

speech   This marks the difference between men and
                     animals, and makes life fuller and more
                     enjoyable. It is the basic form of language,
                     needed for many day-to-day activities, for
                     earning a living, and for getting on with people;
                     it is a major handicap to be deaf or dumb.

Speaking a language is the best way of improving one's knowledge of it; and good writing is usually not far removed from living speech. In some forms of conversation, not very much is communicated; when people chat about the weather or the state of the roads, they do not exchange real information, they just keep on friendly terms as human beings. A more practical form of speech is needed in shopping and at work. Expressive speech conveys our feeling about people, the environment and the lives we lead in it; in this way *dialect* and *slang* have their place (see entries on both). It used to be a disadvantage to use a dialect or speak with a local accent; these are much less of a handicap nowadays, and are sometimes an advantage. But it is useful for speakers of dialect to know Standard English, as the common language of the country and the one taught to all learners, at home or abroad. For practice in spoken English, see Atkinson and Dalton, *The Living Tongue*, and Ch. 6 of Peter Wright, *Language at Work*.

spelling

Learners of English as a second language find this the most difficult part of their task, and some English-speaking people also find it hard. But it is not all-important; those who need the language only for speaking need not trouble much about it. Even when it comes to writing, it is more a social matter than an obstacle to communication, for good spellers may despise bad spellers as uneducated, and an ill-spelled letter of application gives a bad impression of the writer. In examinations only very bad spelling is penalised. People with a serious spelling weakness may be consoled by the facts that Shakespeare spelled his name in several ways – the language was then much more fluid, and consistency in spelling mattered little — and that before his time the same word was sometimes found with different spelling in the same line of writing. Even nowadays in English there are a number of allowable variations — *gray*, *grey* and *learned*, *learnt* are two examples.

There are very few truly hopeless spellers. A number of causes lie behind weak spelling; bad teaching is one, merely telling a child that he or she is a bad speller is another. Sometimes it is a result of a person's going through a difficult phase of life, when he or she is erratic, easily upset, untidy, inconsistent and so on; and it has been proved by experience that when such people settle down, their spelling improves.

Reading is good for spelling, because readers make progress as they become familiar with a good range of words and get to know certain patterns, such as the formation of adverbs by adding *ly*, and various families like the *-age* group: *average*, *damage*, *manage*, *message*, *sausage* and *voyage*.

The important information can be grouped under the headings below. It is best to consult them as the need arises, rather than read them all at once.

1 *Additions to words*

a At the beginning (prefixes)

All loses an *l*, as in *almighty*, *almost*, *alone*, *already*, *also*, *although*, *altogether*, *always*. But *all right* is not — yet — written as one word, so nothing is dropped; and when for our own purposes we prefix a word with *all*, as in *all-conquering*, we can use a hyphen without altering the *all*.

Most prefixes do not change when they are added. For example:

dis+appear becomes disappear

dis+satisfy	,,	dissatisfy
in+accurate	,,	inaccurate
mis+trust	,,	mistrust
mis+spent	,,	misspent
pre+caution	,,	precaution
sub+marine	,,	submarine
un+noticed	,,	unnoticed

ad-	*con-*	*dis-*	*in-*	*sub-*
accommodate	collapse	difference	immoral	suffer
accept	collect	difficulty	immediate	suppose
account	collide		irreligious	support
attract	command		irresponsible	
appearance	correction		illegal	
alliteration				

b At the end (suffixes)

There is no difficulty when *-ly* or *-ness* is added, though if either of them begins with the same letter as that which ends the main word, both parts keep the letter, so that it is doubled:

final+ly becomes finally

thin+ness ,, thinness

Care is needed with *-ed*, *-ing* and other suffixes beginning with a vowel. When one of them is added to a word ending in a single consonant, the consonant is doubled if the syllable is stressed. Thus:

slim	slimming
occur	occurred
begin	beginning
refer	referred

mad	maddening
transmit	transmitter

The doubling of the consonant seems natural, to enable the syllable to take the weight of the stress. But when the last syllable of the main word is not stressed, there is no need to double the final consonant; the suffix is added without change:

focus	focusing
benefit	benefited

When these suffixes beginning with a vowel are added to words ending with a silent *e*, like *give*, the *e* is normally dropped, as in

hope	hoping
like	likable

The important exception is that the silent *e* is kept when it is necessary to show the softly pronounced *g* or *c* in words like *changeable*, *singeing* and *peaceable*. It is also kept in words like *dyeing*, to avoid confusion with *dying* (about to die).

There are some additions that cause no trouble. When -*ment* is added to *argue*, the *e* at the end is dropped; *argument*. This is fairly important; leaving that *e* in is one of the commonest mistakes made by people who usually spell accurately. With *judgment* you can please yourself about the *e* after *g*, though it seems best to drop it, and then it is consistent with *argument*. When -*hood* and -*ness* are added to words ending in *y*, the *y* becomes *i*:

lively	livelihood
busy	business (a very commonly mis-spelled word)

Remember the single *l* in words like *careful* and *grateful*. And without trying to fit them in to a set of rules, bear in mind *daily*, *duly*, *truly*, *wholly*, *awful*, *width*, *ninth* and *original*. They are not difficult words, but people who can spell sometimes make mistakes with them, though they see at once what is wrong if their mis-spelling is queried.

With the endings *-ise*, *-ize* there should be no trouble, unless one wishes to argue about them. The authorities and the big printers, who have their own rules in these matters, do not agree on which alternative should be used, and when. Meanwhile it is perfectly safe to use the *-ise* ending. *See* **-ise, -ize.**

At the same time we should consider the few words that can end in *-ce* or *-se*; here the spellings are positively not alternatives, because the meanings differ; the *-se* indicates a verb, *-ce* is kept for nouns, thus:

verb	*noun*	
advise	advice	
license	licence	
practise	practice	(in America *practice* is used for both verb and noun)
prophesy	prophecy	

It is worth noting that a number of words resemble those we have just listed in being able to act as nouns or verbs, but without any change in spelling. The pronunciation varies according to their use as nouns or verbs; in the noun-use the *s* is pronounced like an *s* (or soft *c*, as in ceiling), whereas the *s* sounds like *z* when the word is used as a verb, thus:

close   excuse   grease   house   refuse

2 *'i' before 'e'*

The rule is:

'i' before 'e'

— except after 'c'

if the sound is 'ee'.

Thus: *relief, believe*; but (after *c* with the 'ee' sound) *ceiling, deceit*. There are a few exceptions to this rule, such as *seize, weird, counterfeit*.

3 *Plurals*

Words ending in -o

Nouns in common use that have long been established as English words have their plurals in -*oes*:

cargoes   mosquitoes   potatoes   tomatoes
volcanoes

Words that were originally abbreviations but now exist in their own right have their plural in -*os*:

curios   photos   radios

And words which, though quite common, still seem to keep a little of their foreignness also have their plural in -*os*:

commandos   dynamos   magnetos   solos
stilettos   studios

It is worth remembering those you can eat — *potatoes, tomatoes* — but the others should not be worried over too much. It is not an important matter, and perhaps one day they will all settle down to having their plural in -*oes*.

Words ending in -y.

In nouns ending with a *consonant* + *y*, the *y* changes to *i*, with -*es* for the plural, thus:

babies   ladies   lilies   territories

But nouns ending in a *vowel* + *y* add the *s* without changing, as in:

alloys   buoys   chimneys   convoys   displays
donkeys   galleys   monkeys   turkeys   valleys

Words ending in -f *and* -fe.

There is no rule, though most of them change the *f* into *v* and add *-es*, like:

calf   calves
knife   knives
shelf   shelves
wife   wives

Some keep the *f* when plural, like:

chiefs   proofs   roofs

And writers who feel that their spelling is inconsistent may like to be reminded that English spelling is inconsistent also, for *hoof*, *staff*, and *wharf* can have their plural in *-fs* or *-ves*. See **foreign words**.

4 *Special cases*

The special thing about these groups is that they are often mis-spelled by quite good spellers, through haste or carelessness.

Double consonant neglected

accommodate   annual   apparatus   appearance
arrangement   brilliant   committee   efficient
embarrass   exaggerate   excellent   immediately
occasion   occur   opportunity   possess
possession   possible   succeed   suppress

Single consonant neglected

(i.e. words in which unnecessary doubling may occur)

around   arouse   control   develop   enemy
explanation   familiar   harass   necessary
omit   opinion   origin   prefer   recommend

— and an extra vowel is sometimes inserted in *prove*.

Words with ea *sound*

jealous dealt meant pleasant weather health
wealth — and some others

5 *Spelling families*

Experience shows that one of the soundest and
most reliable methods of improving spelling is
for the writer to think of words in their
'families'. The truth of this is borne out by
research, an example of which is now
quoted:

If we know that in the word 'courteous', the 'e'
is followed by 'ous' not 'us' we are prepared by
our knowledge of precedent to write 'ous' in the
word 'beauteous'. We implicitly associate
structurally similar words. This is because the
probability of words conforming to spelling
precedent is very high, and it is by becoming
familiar with spelling precedents that we become
good spellers. In other words familiarity with a
coding system is half the battle in learning to spell.
    Margaret L. Peters, *Spelling: Caught or Taught?*

Three family groups have already been
introduced: the -*age* ending (*damage*,
manage . . .), the -*al* beginning (*almost*,
already . . .) and the keeping of *e* before *able* to
indicate pronunciation (*changeable*,
manageable . . .). If the attention of a weak
speller is called to a mistake, it will be worth his
while to see if the word concerned is to be
found in one of the families, and then to read
aloud all the words contained in it.

-*ar ending*

calendar   circular   grammar   particular
regular   salary   sugar

c silent

ascent   crescent   descent   discipline
muscle   scent   scene   schedule   scientist
scissors

c like s

city centre concern criticise deceit and other '-ceit' words defence mercy parcel recent

ch like k

character chemist chorine choir chorus scheme Christian stomach technical ache

eigh sound

eight deign freight feign weigh reign weight

-ence ending

convenience experience preference difference occurrence reference

-fin- words

with root meaning 'boundary', including a word very commonly mis-spelled

affinity finish confine finite define infinite definite refine fine

gu = hard g

disguise guard guerilla guess guide guild guilt guinea guitar intrigue league rogue tongue vague vogue

-or endings

author councillor debtor inspector prospector radiator refrigerator solicitor supervisor surveyor tractor tutor

See -er, or.

other endings

captain certain dictation dubious fountain invention mountain porous relation station treacherous vigorous

6 *Pronunciation helps*

The cause of some mis-spelling is bad or slovenly pronunciation, faults to which most of us are liable. The sentence 'I must have picked the wrong one' is pronounced in a way that is usually written 'I must've picked the wrong one'; but it can all too easily be written 'I must of . . .' by writers who fail to connect what they say with what they see. It is a help to weak spellers to take every opportunity of saying aloud words which cause them difficulty, reading them off a page or list.

First a short selection of one-syllable words, in which the addition of silent *e* to a consonant-vowel-consonant word makes a word with a different meaning and different pronunciation. Verbs have been chosen so that we can see at the same time what happens to them when *-ing* is added:

bar (barring)   bare (baring)
hop (hopping)   hope (hoping)
mat (matting)   mate (mating)
mop (mopping)   mope (moping)
rat (ratting)   rate (rating)
sit (sitting)   site (siting)
tap (tapping)   tape (taping)

Next, correct pronunciation of words ending in *-tion* ('shun') will prevent confusion with words ending in *-sion* ('zhun'):

completion   delusion   effusion   erosion
exclusion   fraction   ignition   profusion
question   suggestion   traction   transfusion

And lastly in this section a list of words that are very commonly mis-spelled by people who have only to say them aloud and carefully to get them right:

actually   amateur   architect   arctic   athletic

comparative competitive cruel depth
different district duel education family
February fuel generally government
gradually introduce laboratory length
library lightning mathematics mischievous
picture probably quietly real recognise
relatives remember responsibility separate
surprise

7 A small group of words in which correct
spelling is helped by thinking about the way in
which they are formed:

because disorder dissect, etc. holiday
misprint mis-spelled, etc. ordered
something sometime they're uneatable
unnecessary, etc. wasn't

Recommendations

It is important not to worry about spelling. It
usually comes right enough in time, if the
person really wants to improve; and I do not
know of anyone whose career has been badly
hampered by poor achievement in this direction.

Some readers may find that this recipe is
helpful with particular words:

a Look at the word carefully; note its syllables
and say it aloud with careful pronunciation.
b Shut your eyes and try to get a mental picture
of the word.
c Check that in your mental picture the spelling
is right.
d Write down the word from memory.
e If difficulty persists, note it down in your own
small dictionary of troublesome words.

Reading aloud helps a learner to associate the
word as written with the spoken word, and is a
most valuable aid. So every opportunity should
be taken, and more opportunities made, of

reading aloud, to the family, children, blind people . . .

Do not put too many words in your private spelling dictionary. Do not try to learn too many words at one go. The rule for learning by heart is: little and often — say five minutes daily. This is more useful, even in a train or bus, than a single hour every week.

split infinitive   Examples of the infinitive form of a verb are *to eat*, *to read*, etc. The term *split infinitive* is used for the separation of *to* from its verb by an adverb, as in:

to quickly eat
to slowly read

On the whole the split infinitive should be avoided. But if it makes better sense to put the adverb in the middle of the infinitive, then by all means let it go there:

I'm anxious to really believe in ghosts.

spoonerisms   These are mistakes in speech of the kind said to have been made frequently by William Spooner, dean of New College, Oxford, who died in 1930. Losing his hat in the High Street on a windy day, he said:

Will nobody pat my hiccup?

And when delivering a sermon to a very small congregation:

It's beery work talking to empty wenches.

Lastly, someone who asked what was on the menu received the answer: Greeks au Latin.

stories   *See* **narrative**.

style   This is a word applied to the way in which any message is expressed. For example, we can say:

There won't be enough dry batteries.

or:

The position with regard to the supply of dry batteries is certain to deteriorate in the near future.

Everyone has his own style of speaking and writing, because everyone has his own ideas and feelings and beliefs. Style cannot be laid on from the outside, like paint. It comes from the way in which a writer is influenced by three factors. First, the content of what he has to say. An account of an escape from a car caught by a river in full flood will be different in style from an account of the same river in a geography book. Secondly, the person or persons to whom the message is addressed will cause the style to be at one extreme chatty and familiar, as in a letter to a relative, and at the other cool and formal, as in an official report. Thirdly, the occasion may make a difference; a gossip round the fire at home or in a pub will encourage a different kind of speech from that needed in a public hall or political meeting.

If you have something to say and really want to say it, the style will look after itself; there are people who cannot read or write who can tell a story or give a description in a style that is just right for the purpose. In a narrative the order of events settles a good deal; in an explanation the logical order of action to be taken acts as a guide. In a description it is best to visualise the subject, and record the most interesting and important material without exaggeration; it is very easy to pile on the adjectives and comparisons. Avoid humour, as a general rule; be sparing with slang and colloquialism; do not use abbreviations. Reading your own work aloud to yourself is not only a useful check on spelling and punctuation, but a means of catching oneself being pompous or pretentious.

See **affectation; business English; cliché; gobbledygook; inflated English; slang; verbosity**.

subject   The *subject* is italicised in each of these sentences:

Gerry has gone home.

The *job* will be finished on time.

What you feel about the holiday matters a lot.

She disagrees.

Note the italicised pronouns in examples below; they are in the nominative case, because they are part of the subject of the verb. Some students make the mistake of putting these pronouns in the accusative case.

Jane and *I* were first off the coach.

Her friends and *we* three queued for tickets.

Who do you think will be there?

David and *he* won their events.

See **case; nominative**.

subject, choosing a
         See **essay writing; material**.

subject, multiple
         When the subject of a sentence consists of more than one item, the verb must be plural. Examples of these multiple subjects and the verbs that go with them are italicised in these sentences:

He and *I were* right after all.

Eliot and *Harvey are expected* to be in the first five.

What you think and *what you do are* two very different things.

Occasionally groups of words have been closely connected for so long that they are regarded as a unit; and then they take a singular verb. Here are some examples of such 'parcel' expressions:

Bacon and eggs is always on the menu.
'Plain Tales from the Hills' is on my book-list.
Whisky and soda costs too much nowadays.

There is no hard-and-fast rule, and in many cases either a singular or plural verb will fit:

Pen and wash is/are this artist's favourite medium.

See **agreement; collective nouns**.

subordinate

This is a grammatical term used to describe what every user of language does without thinking. In the expression:

We had no money left *and* we went home a day early.

the two halves joined by *and* are grammatically of equal importance. But if we alter it to read:

Since we had no money left, we went home a day early.

we have made the first part subordinate to the second. There is now only one main verb, *went*; and the verb *had* is part of a subordinate clause. The term *subordinate* need not be learned; the important thing is to use subordinate clauses when they make the meaning clearer.

such

In the sentence:

Many famous pictures can be seen in Italian galleries, such as Botticelli's 'Primavera'

the meaning is not clearly expressed; as it stands, it means that *Botticelli's 'Primavera'* is a gallery. The remedy is to place the *such as* . . . clause next to the word it qualifies – in this case, *pictures*:

Many famous pictures, such as Botticelli's 'Primavera', can be seen in Italian galleries.

suffixes   Most nouns in English can be used as adjectives:

spring fashions
summer frocks
autumn sales
winter woollies

but if we need to separate the adjective from its noun we have to make up an adjective by an addition, or *suffix*, and say:

The weather is spring-*like*.
Now the days are summer*y*.
The trees look autumn*al*.
The sky is win*try*.

Suffixes can convert verbs into nouns: *deny* becomes *denial*; they make adjectives out of nouns: *origin* becomes *original*; verbs out of nouns: *glory*, *glorify*. Here are some examples of suffixes:

suffix	*meaning*	*examples*
-able, -ible	able to, capable of being	audible, eatable
-al	connected with . . .	fatal, trial
-er	one who . . ., that which . . .	player, cooker
-ess	female	waitress, lioness
-ful	full of . . ., full, filled	joyful, spoonful
-fy	make	simplify, unify
-graphy	writing about . . ., pictures	topography, photography
-hood	the quality of . . .	girlhood, manhood
-ise	make	antagonise, vulcanise
-less	without, lacking	hopeless, weightless

-ology	study of . . .	biology, geology
-ous	with the quality of . . ., full of . . .	famous, dangerous
-meter	measure for . . .	speedometer, thermometer
-ship	the quality of . . ., position of . . .	workmanship, stewardship

See **opposites, spelling, 1**.

summaries

There is very little difference between a summary and a précis; and many books regard them as one and the same. In practice however we can make a distinction. A précis is a reduced version of the original, like something made small by viewing through the wrong end of a telescope. A summary often takes the form of selecting particular arguments, the evidence for one side of a case, or special aspects of a situation. For example, in an examination a long article about the provision of driving lessons in school may be printed; and the candidate may be asked to summarise the arguments in favour of giving such tuition in schools. If so, he will have to neglect the other material. A précis on the other hand would give a shortened version of the whole, including the arguments against learning to drive at school. As usual, it is a matter of reading the question carefully and then providing what is asked for. *See* **précis**.

symbols

These are a form of shorthand. There are visual symbols, like the Cross which stands for Christianity, and the hammer and sickle for communism. To save space, dictionaries use symbols — a horizontal arrow, for instance, means *look at*; and in biology there are special symbols for male and female. In speech and writing they are common; we often read in the newspapers about 'hawks' and 'doves', meaning people and parties who are for or against the use of military force. These expressions convey their meaning to us because hawks are symbols of violent action, whereas a dove is always a symbol of peace. Other words that often have a symbolic meaning (suggested in brackets) are: gold (wealth); star (permanence, remoteness); seed (life); fountain (fertility, life); and autumn (old age).

synonyms

The term applied to two or more words with much the same meaning, as for example: *affectionate, loving; fatigued, weary, tired; odour, smell; surrender, yield.* But it is very rare indeed for two words to have exactly the same meaning; if it does happen, the tendency is for one to drop completely out of use and be totally forgotten. When there is a slight difference in meaning, both words in a pair of synonyms survive, because both are useful. For instance, in our first pair, *loving* is a little stronger, a little deeper than *affectionate*. In the next group, *fatigued* has a slightly technical note, and is likely to be found in a book on health or medicine; while *weary* is a stage beyond being *tired*. How does one decide which of several synonyms should be used? The precise shade of meaning required is one factor, the person or persons addressed is another, and the occasion (an examination paper or a chat with a friend) is a third. They add up to the complete context, and with practice users of English come to select the right word automatically without taking thought. In English dialects there are – or used to be – 1,300 ways of telling a person he is a fool, about 1,050 words for a slattern and 120 titles for the smallest pig of a litter. If quite uneducated people could light on the right word at the right time, we with all our education ought to do at least as well. Moreover, we have good dictionaries, and they are a great help with synonyms. *See* **shades of meaning**.

syntax

This is the word applied to the rules for constructing sentences, but no one ever built a good sentence through only knowing the rules. The best way to make good sentences is practice with a purpose, backed up by hearing a variety of sentence patterns in conversation, over the air, and in print.

T

-t, -ed

The following words can have their past tense and their past participle in either *-ed* or *-t*:

burn	burned	burnt
dream	dreamed	dreamt
kneel	kneeled	knelt
lean	leaned	leant
leap	leaped	leapt
learn	learned	learnt
smell	smelled	smelt
spell	spelled	spelt
spill	spilled	spilt
spoil	spoiled	spoilt

tabulation

This is a useful way of setting out statistics or lists of items; for examples, see the entry immediately before this one, and the entry on *suffixes*. The place for tabulation is in writing about science, geography and so on; there is not much scope for the device in English essays.

tact

This costs only a little thought; and in an overcrowded world it helps to make people's dealings with each other go more smoothly. It was no help to a person who had lost a relative to receive from the insurance company concerned a letter that included the sentence:

'We look forward to receiving the death certificate'.

tautology

This is the technical term for needless repetition; the italicised words in the following expressions merely repeat an idea already present in the other word:

and etc.
co-operate *together*
final completion
joint partnership
meet *up with*
prejudge *in advance*

See **redundant words**.

technical terms

These are the groups of words used in pursuing a particular craft, hobby, science, trade, profession or branch of learning. A layman is one without the special skill or knowledge belonging to these pursuits. Most people are laymen at one time, experts at another. An engineer is a layman when music or cooking are being discussed, whereas cooks and musicians are usually laymen when an engineering topic comes up. In conversation and writing technical terms should be used sparingly, and then with an explanation. Too many of them can make the hearer or reader feel out of it. *See* **jargon**.

tense

There are three *tenses*, present, past and future, and each has three types:

	Present	*Past*	*Future*
Simple	I think	I thought	I shall think
Continuous	I am thinking	I was thinking	I shall be thinking
Perfect	I have thought	I had thought	I shall have thought

than   This word is rightly used after a comparative adjective or adverb:

My car is an *older* model *than* yours.
An electric hedge cutter does the job much *quicker than* a man could.

It should not be used after words like *prefer*, *choose*, *option*; in these examples the correct word is in brackets:

Do you prefer wallpaper than (*to*) emulsion paint?
We had no option than (*but*) to pay the bill.

that   As a relative pronoun this word is used only in *defining* clauses:

This is the house *that* Jack built

Here the relative clause picks out a particular house, and works very like an adjective; if it is omitted, the four words left do not make much sense. For contrast we print a non-defining clause:

Modern houses, which normally have cavity walls, tend to be better insulated.

Here the clause beginning *which* could be left out of the sentence without destroying the sense. The difference between the two types of clause is perhaps not a vital one for learners, since the correct usage comes automatically as the student makes general progress in his knowledge of language.

The use of *that* in such sentences as:

The more that I see of invalid cars, the less I like them

is incorrect; the remedy is just to omit *that*.

theirselves   Officially there is no such word, and we should use *themselves*, as in:

They hurt themselves on the barbed wire.

See **pronouns, 1**.

theme sentence *See* **paragraph**.

thing   This word suffers from overwork. Students who
                   find themselves using it too often should try for
                   a more exact word that tells us more and fits
                   better into the context. Here are some examples
                   of the overworked *thing*, with improved
                   versions in brackets:

                   I bought a *thing* for grinding coffee (I bought a
                   coffee mill).

                   What a good *thing* it would be if we could get
                   on the road by six (What a help it would be . . .).

                   Labour-saving *things* (devices).

                   Things like cup-ties don't happen every day
                   (Events).

this   There has come from America an odd use of
                   this adjective, of which an example is given in
                   the quotation in the *time* entry; please look it up.
                   The reader's or hearer's reaction is likely to be
                   'Which bar? Which guy? You haven't mentioned
                   either before, so how can you refer to them like
                   this?' *This* is a demonstrative adjective; it is used
                   to point to something actually visible or just
                   mentioned. In standard English *a* would be used
                   instead of *this* in the example just referred to.
                   However some authorities strongly defend the
                   use of *this* as just described.

thought   Good writing depends on good thinking.
                   Therefore even a short letter should be planned,
                   in the mind at least, before it is written. With
                   longer pieces of work, always jot down a
                   scheme of some kind, to get the facts in the
                   right order and arguments in logical form. The
                   act of preparing to write often helps to clear up

one's mind; it assists the writer to reach a detached point of view and take a fresh look at facts that may be doubtful and arguments that may be unsound.

through   Do not abbreviate this word in written work.

time   Stories and narratives are usually told in the past tense, but for the sake of vividness some episodes are put in the present tense, especially at the climax of a story. In conversation too the present is often used:

I goes into this bar, see, and this guy offers me a drink, and I get talking and we play darts an hour or two.

Speakers sometimes mix up the times at which things happen:

We *stroll* around the shops till evening and then we all *went* into the disco.

But in writing, unnecessary shifts in time should be avoided; they can produce real muddles if used carelessly.

titles   Titles of books, films, plays and names of ships are printed in *italics*; in writing and typing they are underlined. Anything from a book, like the heading of a chapter, subject of a section, or a poem, should go in single quotation marks:

'Smoke and Steel' is the best section of Sandburg's *Harvest Poems*.

transitive   If you look up a verb in a dictionary, the definition is likely to start with one of:

vt   vi

v stands for *verb*, *t* for *transitive*, *i* for *intransitive*. If both *vt* and *vi* are given, the verb can be either *transitive* or *intransitive*. *Transitive* verbs

stand for actions that affect something
mentioned in the sentence concerned, as in:

Has the dog *eaten* its *dinner*?

The cat *snatched it*.

Explain *what you're doing*.

Intransitive verbs have no object:

Here I *am*.

The birds *are singing*.

They'll *sleep* when the sun *sets*.

**And here are examples of verbs that can be
either *transitive* or *intransitive*:**

The clock *ticked* quietly. (intransitive)

She *ticked the items* on her shopping list.
(transitive)

We *parked* in the multi-storey. (intransitive)

They've *parked that car* awkwardly. (transitive)

**It is useful to know these terms, as they are
commonly used by teachers. *See* object.**

try and   Some authorities argue that this expression
should never be used, and that we should
always say and write *try to*, as in:

Try to do better.

But there is a slight difference in meaning. 'Try
and do better' is encouraging: 'Try – and you'll
do better'. 'Try to do better' is much more of a
command.

U

un-, in-   This is the commonest of the negative prefixes:
unhurt, unbelievable, undone. In most cases it
becomes part of the word it negatives, so that
there is no hyphen; but when the main word

begins with a capital letter a hyphen must be used, as in: *un-British, un-Christian*.

It is stronger than the prefix *non-*. If we say that a person is *non-British* we merely mean that he is of a different nationality. But if we declare that an act or attitude is *un-British* we show our strong disapproval of it. Similarly with *non-Christian*, which means exactly what it says: not Christian. But *un-Christian* implies something positively opposed to what is Christian, and undesirable:

It was an un-Christian act to sue a poor widow for a debt of 10p.

The prefix *in-* is the strongest negative, as we can see in the word *inedible*, which means quite unfit for eating and possibly poisonous. Whereas *uneatable* suggests only that a substance is ill-cooked, unpleasant in flavour or difficult to digest — not that it is dangerous. *See also* **in-, un-**.

underlining   In writing or typing, underlining indicates that the word or phrase should be printed in italics. *See* **italics**.

**under-
statement**

If someone who has swum the Channel is asked by a stranger what his hobby is, the reply might be, 'Oh, I do a bit of swimming sometimes'. That would be an *understatement*. Such expressions as the swimmer's are the result of modesty, the wish not to appear boastful; they are thought to be characteristically English. They can also be applied to extreme situations, as the best way of bringing home a truth. A person who has had a very painful operation in hospital might say about it: 'It wasn't exactly pleasant'. Lastly, understatement can be useful when a speaker wishes to be kind or to scale down a person's weakness or imperfection. For example, a very fat person may be described as a *trifle overweight*, or a deaf person as *rather hard of hearing*.

uninterested   *See* **disinterested**.

us or we   *We* is the nominative case of the first person plural; *us* is the objective case. There is no difficulty when *we* is the only subject of a verb — *we agree* — or when *us* is the object of a verb; *They followed us*. But some people have trouble with multiple subjects or objects. In these sentences *we* and *us* are correctly used:

Owing to the strike the Johnsons and *we* had to walk home. (subject)

But the Smiths took the Johnsons and *us* in their car. (object)

See **case; object; subject**.

usage   This word is applied to a form of language that has become accepted through long use. For example:

Who are you going with?

is now accepted as normal. But grammatically it is incorrect; strictly speaking we ought to say *With whom are you going?* However, anyone who did say that could sound pedantic; and the experts on language believe that *whom* is on the way out.

used to   This expression sometimes trips speakers up when it is negatived or turned into a question. Here are the correct forms, with a common error in brackets for identification:

Positive: I used to type my own letters.

Negative: I used not to type my own letters (NOT: I didn't use to . . .)

Question: Did you use to type your own letters?

V

variety

A piece of writing can be intelligible and clear in its meaning, and yet be rather dull and heavy to read. One reason for this may be the repetition of a word where an alternative would provide variety and brighten things up. Here are three examples of tedious repetition from the work of one student writer:

Steve *made* a cup of tea while we *made* the last checks before setting course for Jupiter. (Replace the second *made* by *carried out*.)

The main character lives in a *country* style house in the *country*. (It is not clear what *country style* indicates. Omit.)

A *large* cylinder embedded in the ground was watched by a *large* crowd. (There are plenty of synonyms for *large*.)

See **repetition**.

verbs, form of   The important forms of some common verbs are:

Present	Past	Past Participle	Present	Past	Past Participle
am	was	been	get	got	got
bear	bore	borne	give	gave	given
become	became	become	go	went	gone
begin	began	begun	grow	grew	grown
break	broke	broken	keep	kept	kept
bring	brought	brought	lead	led	led
buy	bought	bought	know	knew	known
catch	caught	caught	lay	laid	laid
choose	chose	chosen	leave	left	left
come	came	come	lie	lay	lain
do	did	done	lose	lost	lost
drink	drank	drunk	make	made	made
eat	ate	eaten	meet	met	met
fall	fell	fallen	pay	paid	paid
feel	felt	felt	rise	rose	risen

say	said	said	speak	spoke	spoken
seek	sought	sought	think	thought	thought
sell	sold	sold	write	wrote	written
send	sent	sent			

See **active and passive; agreement; double past tense; -ed, -t; finite and infinite; imperative; transitive; main verb; sentences; singular and plural; split infinitive; subject, multiple; tense.**

verbiage, verbosity

The use of too many words or too long words, where brevity would be more effective. Here are some examples, with suggested improvements in brackets:

a considerable amount of	(much)
as to whether	(whether)
at this moment of time	(now)
cost effective	(economical)
I would also add that	(omit the words)
in this day and age	(nowadays)
only too glad	(glad)
until such time as	(until)

See **business English; clichés; gobbledygook; inflated English; redundancy; dignity words; woolliness.**

very

This word is sometimes overworked, and when used (for instance) at the rate of four times in four lines of writing, it loses its strength. The re-reading of one's work will usually reveal excessive use. When this happens, consider first if the words are really wanted; and if they are, seek alternatives for some of the *verys*, such as *exceedingly, exceptionally, noticeably, completely, remarkably* and so on. *See* **intensifiers**.

vogue words These are terms that come into fashion and flourish for a time. They are usually meant to impress the reader or hearer; they are quite frequently used without a knowledge of their true meaning, like the second and last of these samples, current at the time of writing:

ambivalent   catalyst   involvement
meaningful   protagonist   streamlined   top-level
viable

vowels The letters *a, e, i, o* and *u* are used, sometimes singly, sometimes in pairs, in the written versions of the various vowel sounds heard in English speech. The letter *y* can also act as a vowel.

W

what This word can take a singular or a plural verb, according to the context. In this example:

Get some more milk; what we have *is* not enough for three.

the verb is goes into the singular because *milk* is singular. But in:

Any more suitcases? No, what we have *are* all here.

the verb *are* is plural because *suitcases* is plural. In another example:

What we want for refugees *is* hot water bottles.

the verb *is* is correct, because the idea of *want* is singular. But the common usage is to say and write *are* in such sentences, and it very much looks as if usage is winning the fight against correctness.

when, where These words are sometimes used wrongly, especially in definitions:

Malnutrition *is when* a person has inadequate food over a long period.

The verb *is* could be strengthened to *develops* or *occurs*, and then the sentence will be correct.

Smog *is where* poisonous exhaust gases from cars collect over towns.

Here again the verb *is* should be changed to *is found, collects, is formed*. Or the sentence can be re-cast:

Smog consists of poisonous exhaust gases from cars, which collect over towns.

The 'wrong' sentences are intelligible, but they are not good English.

whether, if   The word *if* often replaces *whether*; and some authorities object to its use in this way:

They asked *if* the flight recorder had survived the crash.

But there is no doubt that *if* in this sense has come to stay, especially since it supplies a shade of meaning that is not conveyed by *whether*. If the reader of this page were to collect examples of his or her own use of *if* in place of *whether*, he or she would find that *if* was always chosen when the speaker wished the event he was enquiring about to happen, as in in these examples:

He asked *if* tea was ready.

Let me know *if* there's anything in the paper about our concert.

If there is a negative alternative, *whether* must be used:

They asked the clerk *whether* their tickets were available or not.

while   The word is often used as a change from *and*:

Joan Brett was elected Chairman and Mrs. French vice-chairman, *while* Sylvia Jones became treasurer.

However there have been some slips involving odd simultaneous actions:

The vicar preached the sermon, *while* Mr Day read the lesson.

While can also be used to mean much the same as *although*:

While I disagree with them, I do think your points are well worth making.

which

This relative pronoun is applied to things, never people:

I use special film *which* can't be bought in ordinary shops.

who

This is used for people and sometimes for favourite animals:

People *who've* finished please hand in their answers.

Miss Burrows was always accompanied by Meg, *who* had been her guide dog for ten years.

whom

This word will not be in use much longer, but grammar books still try to insist that *who* should be replaced by *whom* in these examples:

Who are you looking for?

Who are you going with?

I can't think who we'll choose.

In speech the use of *whom* would sound affected, and it would be out of place in all but the most formal writing.

whose

This is normally applied to persons, as in the first example below, but it is more and more used of things, as in the second example:

Drivers *whose* licences have expired must apply for renewal.

There are very few clubs *whose* membership is increasing.

For *which, who, whom, whose see* **pronouns, 3.**

will   *See* **shall, will.**

without   This is commonly used in conversation instead of *unless*:

I won't go on the river *without* you come too.

But it is sub-standard English, and is best avoided in writing.

woolliness   An examiner's report complained: 'It is a pity that too many candidates muffled their thoughts in words which have become so hackneyed as to be practically without meaning. Such words as "factor, trend, avenue, field, facet, situation" were used rather like crutches to help a limping writer; they certainly did not convey thought'.

Here is an example from an examination paper:

The author mentions zest to let it reflect on how much drive education had in its pure state on the people and how much it would then be useless as an incentive at all.

It is difficult to extract any meaning from this writing. It is not an extreme case, for thousands of them occur every year. This woolliness in writing shows that the writers do not know what they want to say; they have not thought enough, nor have they had practice enough. *See* **verbiage.**

words   **1** *Choice*

With its enormous vocabulary English offers a range of words for what appears to be a single meaning. For example:

I saw someone/an individual/a man/a person/ a stranger in the crowd waving/gesticulating/ signalling/trying to attract my attention/making signs.

Normally the shortest and easiest word is best, provided that it is the most exact for the meaning intended; *begin* is better than *commence*, *finish* than *terminate*. But sometimes the context in which the word is used will require a longer word; a technical term may be needed, or a special word from the vocabulary of (say) the medical or legal profession may be the right one. If a writer really thinks out what he has to say, the right word will appear and fall into its place. *See* **shades of meaning; synonyms.**

2 *Easily confused*

The following words are liable to be mis-used:

accede, exceed
affect, effect
complement, compliment
contemptible, contemptuous
continual, continuous
credible, credulous
eligible, illegible
explicit, implicit
industrial, industrious
infer, imply

innocuous, innocent
lightening, lightning
luxuriant, luxurious
negligent, negligible
official, officious
practice, practise
principal, principle
recourse, resource
sociable, social
stationary, stationery
uninterested, disinterested

3 *Foreign*

English has borrowed with profit a large number of words and phrases from other languages. Here is a selection of them:

à la carte   anorak   apartheid   au pair   circa
cul de sac   data   de facto   ex officio

fait accompli   impasse   in camera
inter alia   karate   modus operandi   moped
ombudsman   pro tem   quasi   quid pro quo
status quo   ultra vires   viva voce   volte face

would, should   These words are the past forms of *will* and *shall*;
please consult the entry *'shall', 'will'*. They can
also be used to make a polite request or a
rather mild suggestion:

Would you mind opening the window, please?

I should take a mac, if I were you.

There used to be a fashion for saying 'I
wouldn't know', when all the speaker meant
was 'I don't know'. The expression seems to be
lapsing at present; there is no point in keeping it
alive. Similarly it is better to say 'I think' rather
than 'I would think'.

Y

you and I   Mistakes are rarely made with the normal:

You and I are sharing the same room again.

I is nominative because it is part of the subject
of the verb *are sharing*; and *are* is plural because
it has a double subject, *You and I*. But this is
what happens with *either . . . or, neither . . . nor*:

Neither you nor I am leaving.

The conjunctions *neither . . . nor* cause *you* and
I to be regarded separately, one at a time; so the
verb is singular. Then we have *you* in the
second person, and *I* in the first person; when
this happens the person of the verb is decided
by the pronoun nearest to it. The verb is
therefore *am leaving*. But it must be admitted
that most English people, however well
educated, would say *are leaving* without
hesitation. *See* **subject, multiple**.

Note that in *between you and me*, the pronoun *me* goes in the objective cause because it is governed by the preposition *between*.

yours   A too common error is to insert an apostrophe between the *r* and the *s*. Anyone in doubt on this point should consult the entry *apostrophe*, to make sure when apostrophes have to be added.